GW01315913

Also by Matthew Woodward:

Trans-Siberian Adventures
A Bridge Even Further
The Railway to Heaven
Silver Streak

Bang Sue Junction
Adventures in Thailand by Train
Matthew Woodward

Caroline,

This is our fifth book!

My very best

Matthew

LANNA HALL PUBLISHING

A LANNA HALL BOOK

First published in Great Britain in 2023
by Lanna Hall Publishing

Copyright © 2023 Matthew Woodward

Matthew Woodward has asserted his right
under the Copyright, Designs and Patents Act
1988 to be identified as the author of this work.
Every reasonable effort has been made to
contact copyright holders of material reproduced
in this book. If any have been overlooked, the
publisher would be glad to hear from them and
make good in future editions any errors or
omissions brought to their attention.
All rights reserved. No part of this publication
may be reproduced, stored in a retrieval system,
or transmitted in any form or by any means,
electronic, mechanical, photocopying, recording
or otherwise, without the prior permission of the
copyright owner.

ISBN 979 8 86265 824 8

Cover design and illustrations by Josh Gibson
Edited by Caroline Petherick

www.matthew-woodward.com

'I'm not a trainspotter, I'm a railway enthusiast.'

Eric Lomax, author of The Railway Man

Contents

	Introduction	9
1.	Bang Sue Junction	17
2.	Outbreak	21
3.	Nana	33
4.	Man on Fire	51
5.	Bridge on the River Kwai	67
6.	The Blues Brothers	79
7.	Into the Heart of Darkness	85
8.	The Big Mango	107
9.	Combat Rock	117
10.	Elephant Man	133
11.	Trainspotting	159
12.	The Delicate Sound of Thunder	169
13.	The Railway People	187
14.	Cool Hand Matthew	197
15.	Heavy Metal	219
	Afterword	231
	Glossary	235
	Acknowledgements	237
	About the Author	241

Introduction

I like the idea that the origins of the railway in Thailand might have been inspired by a model train set. It had been a gift to the King of Siam from Queen Victoria in 1855. Prince Chulalongkorn, later King Rama V, would have been just three years old when the crate arrived in the royal court, and I'm sure that he would have been fascinated by the intricacies of the steam engine, and absorbed thoughts of its possibilities in the real world.

I first travelled through Thailand by train on my way to Singapore in the winter of 2014. I remember it being the winter, as I'd had a brutally cold crossing of Siberia before heading south. Arriving at Poipet on the Cambodian/Thai border, I caught one of the twice-daily third-class trains from the nearby station at Aranyaprathet to Bangkok, and from there I took a train known as the International Express. At that time this was a daily cross-border service connecting Bangkok with Butterworth in Malaysia. These two train journeys delivered all of the best train travel clichés; sights, sounds, and smells – mostly good ones – that embed the experience of life on the rails in Thailand. I knew right then that I would be back for more.

I feel that I must apologise that I have become someone who regards railway modernisation with mild suspicion. So many grand stations and traditions in other countries have been obliterated by more efficient but yet soulless advancements. Thailand, however, currently has one of the most enjoyable railways that I have ever come across. Whilst I'm sure it will be exciting to travel all the way from China to Singapore directly by high-speed rail in the future, I have learned on my travels that speed isn't everything, and the experience may not be the huge leap forward that people imagine. Of course, I realise that efficiency will preserve one of the main purposes of train travel, but my hope is that the old and the new will be able to run side by side for many years to come.

If you find yourself embarking on a rail adventure in Thailand you have to be quite careful with names and places. It's quite normal for a station to have more than one name, and for the

Introduction

locals to use a name that's different to the one that is printed on your ticket. Bangkok Railway Station, or Krunthep Station, is the official name for perhaps the most well-known station in the kingdom, Hua Lamphong. And *that* is technically the name for a station close by, which closed in 1960. Likewise, its smaller cousin across the river has been renamed Thonburi,[1] but many locals still call it Bangkok Noi, the name for another nearby station that was once on the bank of the Chao Phraya River. It keeps you on your toes. Bangkok is also now the home to what will soon become the largest railway station in South East Asia. At the time of writing it has a massive illuminated sign on its frontage proclaiming its name as Bang Sue Grand. But its name has already been changed. It is now officially known as Krung Thep Aphiwat Central Terminal Station. I suspect taxi drivers might be calling it something simpler for some time to come.

I have been asked about the choice of title for this book. Bang Sue is a central suburban district in the city. Contrary to some Western jokes, there is no one called Sue involved in this story. In fact, the word *bang* means 'area by the river'; Bang Sue can be translated as 'community of faithful', and

---

[1] or Thon Buri; both forms are used

Bangkok, 'olive grove by the river'. Bang Sue was one of the city's original stations.

I have done my best to keep things as clear and consistent as possible with names and translations, but if you find yourself confused at any point, please have a look at the glossary towards the back of the book.

A brief word on health and safety. Thai people are often left to make their own informed choices about what constitutes danger in their everyday lives. Railways and people don't always mix well, and every year there are unfortunate accidents for all sorts of reasons. Some of them are wholly preventable whilst others are caused by someone just being in the wrong place at the wrong time. By Western standards, some of my experiences involved taking a calculated degree of risk; as they say, please don't try this at home.

I hope you enjoy this journey on the rails. If you have any children, please give them a model railway. You never know what it might lead to.

Matthew Woodward
Chichester, West Sussex, 2020.

Introduction

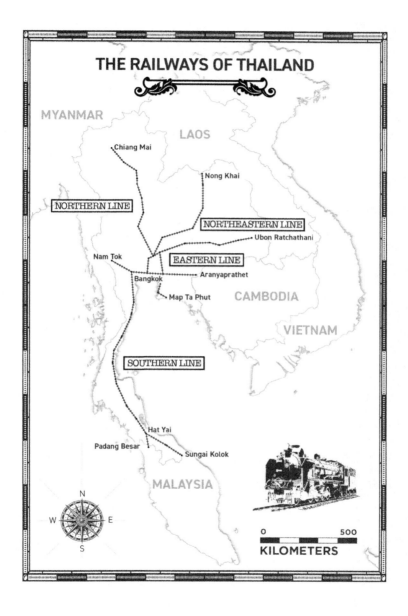

Bang Sue Junction

Introduction

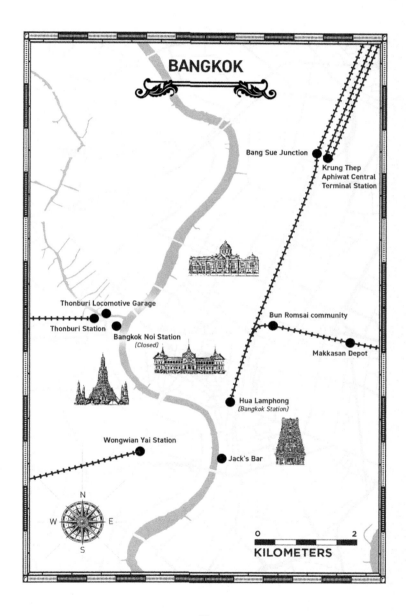

Bang Sue Junction

Chapter One
Bang Sue Junction

It's a steaming hot Bangkok day in May 2022. The stationmaster at Bang Sue Junction has a gleaming brass bell hanging beside his head, and he rings it three times to signal the departure of the local train standing in front of him at Platform 1. The cadence of his dings has both precision and purpose, perfectly matching his well-ironed uniform and highly polished boots. He is controlling time. More precisely, train time. His digital watch is exactly synchronised with the analogue clock on the wall in his office and matched to his encyclopaedic knowledge of the planned departure time of every train at the station. When the sound of the final ding reaches the guard at the front carriage of the train, he waves his flag, signalling to the driver to release the brakes and pull back the throttle of the Alstom diesel locomotive. The train slowly gathers momentum and rumbles out of sight, leaving people up and down the platform to return to what they were doing before it arrived; mostly eating and chatting.

I like to people-watch, and the station platforms of Thailand are a wonderful place to observe the hustle and bustle of everyday life. They are not just places to catch trains, but also restaurants, police stations, botanic gardens and even museums. Their spaces feel more relaxed, safe and friendly than the street outside. There is a quiet order on the platform. Everything is spick and span here. Rocks are whitewashed, and even the thick blades of Asian grass are chopped to a uniform height in the flowerbeds. Most stations feel like a social club, and people are content to sit in the shade and share news. Some might actually be catching a train.

Bang Sue Junction isn't a particularly pretty station by Thai standards, and is certainly not a grand one, but it has been a vital part of the railways of Thailand since its opening in 1898. It was the original Bangkok Station for the very first state-owned railway line, running between Bangkok and Ayutthaya, Siam's ancient capital. Bang Sue wasn't originally a junction at all, but as the rail network expanded it became a vital node connecting long-distance railway lines with the larger and much more impressive Bangkok Railway Station located in the heart of the city.

If you are lucky enough to find an empty seat on Platform 1 you can witness train time travel. But first of all, it's best to find Chompoo, the lady who sells brightly coloured frozen ice drinks towards the southern end of the platform at Bang Sue 2. At one time Bang Sue Junction was actually two stations, each serving different lines, but they have now all been combined here at the second station. Walk past the stationmaster and the monks in their reserved seating area, and you will find Chompoo towards the end of a row of food stalls busy serving hungry workers on their meal break. She has several chopped-up logs that you can sit on whilst you cool off under an improvised tarpaulin sunshade. The lime soda here is pretty good, but I'd recommend asking for one with less sugar. The locomotives that come past your log jump forwards and backwards in time. They pull both old and new carriages to destinations as far away as Chiang Mai in the north, Nong Khai in the north east and Su-ngai Kolok in the deep south. Charming old rickety third-class carriages with open windows intermingle with the latest Chinese-built air-conditioned luxury sleeper coaches. Looking further back in time, you might even spot a pair of Japanese steam locomotives pulling special excursion trains to popular tourist destinations. Whilst this railway has been considerably developed over time, nothing has fundamentally changed over the last century. Nothing, that is, until now.

Take a sip of your frosty drink and peer over the barbecue haze and your eyes will fall upon a very different sort of railway on the other side of the tracks. A vast gleaming curved metal superstructure that appears to go on for almost as far as you can see. It looks more like an airport terminal or even an alien spaceship than a railway station. This is the new Krung Thep Aphiwat Central Terminal Station, which is destined to become the largest station in South East Asia. In just a few years it will provide high-speed rail connections to Laos, China, Malaysia and Singapore. If you look closely at the raised tracks protruding out of the end you might spot a bright shiny new red and grey Ultraman electro-diesel train. You have just travelled from the 19th to the 21st century in a single railway vista.

Chapter Two
Outbreak

I returned from a rail adventure in the United States just a few days before the world became a very different place. The President was being interviewed about the Covid-19 coronavirus on a rolling news channel being screened in the airport lounge. 'It's going to be down to close to zero,' he told the reporter. 'That's a pretty good job we've done. It's going to be close to zero.' I don't remember the exact sequence of events, but it wasn't long before hospital admissions were surging in hotspots around the world. There were emergency flights to repatriate citizens to the country they called home, and then the travel industry shut down. You will have your own memories of these dark times. In the United

Kingdom we were told to 'stay at home to save lives', although it later turned out this didn't apply to everyone.

I found myself ringing bells in the evening and painting rainbows in support of emergency workers. Press briefings ranged from pretty gloomy daily realities to the possibility of a terrifying dystopian future. A new dialect of R numbers, mortality rates and strains became embedded in the news. Fleeting conversations with neighbours in my social bubble were my only contact with people in the outside world, other than my grocery delivery driver, who I greeted in mask and rubber gloves before washing everything in the crate. Then along came Zoom, clever technology that quickly became a monumental chore. As my hair grew longer and longer I felt I could comfortably pass for a former member of a 1970s rock band. Maybe not the lead singer, but definitely the drummer who had let himself go a bit.

The weeks became months and the months became years as waves of the virus swept through the world. Every day the BBC would publish data showing the cases reported right down to the postcode I lived in. One month we were back in the local pub – and the next it was masks back on and stay at home again. Then the miracle of vaccination and the madness of those against it. You could make a movie about it if it hadn't already been made.

Friends would ask me how I was and I'd say that I was okay, but the truth was that I was concerned I might be going doolally being on my own and in one place for so long. I needed a coping strategy, and I decided that this would be to get on with planning my next adventure. In the mornings I would work on the book that became *Silver Streak,* and after some officially permitted outdoor exercise on my bicycle, I would retire to my little library, a room full to the brim with books, maps, artefacts from past expeditions, and a supply of reasonably good sherry.

When I moved house a couple of years ago I found a dusty campaign desk at my local auction house, along with a battered red leather chair. The desk was the type that in the past a senior officer would have taken with him to war, along with his golf clubs and cigars. It took apart into several pieces, and was reinforced with brass bands and handles, for just this purpose. I had no plans to take it to any more wars, though; now in my library, it was stacked high with piles of books. If you are a railway enthusiast like me you probably have a shelf just for railway books. The problem was that mine had been growing considerably since I had been locked up at home. It was beginning to sag under the weight, so my desk had become the holding space until I could decide which of my books were no longer indispensable reading, an almost impossible task.

Whatever the weather outside, with the reading lamp on and the fire burning it felt cosy and comfortable in here, even if a bit Victorian. One miserably wet winter afternoon I fixed myself a pot of tea, and seeking fresh inspiration began to sift through the nearest stack of books at the front of the desk. I needed something to focus my mind on that would take me away from the pandemic and to a much happier place. Sandwiched between the scuffed red cover of a copy of *Bradshaw's Continental Railway Guide* and the pretty blue dust jacket of *Appleton's General Guide to the United States and Canada*, I noticed a book that I had purchased from a dealer in America a few months earlier. The book was thinner than the other books in the pile, but stood out with its dark green cover and ornate gold printed patterns. This was the 1928 *Guide to Bangkok*, published by the Royal State Railways of Siam.

The rain was getting heavier outside, the strong westerly wind driving it across the fields of winter barley and into the exposed side of my house. I settled into my chair, poured a cup of tea and began to read. I quickly became absorbed in the content of its yellowed pages. I loved perusing the vintage adverts for hotels, department stores, jewellers, drinks brands and shipping companies. The advice was also very much of its time. The guide suggested I might arrive by steamer, and not to worry if I didn't have a passport, just visit the Siamese consul on arrival at the port. Once in Bangkok I could then visit the Railway Information Bureau at the Bangkok Railway Terminus during office hours. The telephone number was Railway 549. The *book* had descriptions of each of the rail lines in the country, and suggested itineraries using hotels en route. The late Lord Northcliffe remarked, 'My principal recollections of the Siamese State Railways are of wonderful smoothness of running, of beautiful scenery, and of one of the most peaceful and comfortable train journeys I can remember.'

I imagined myself wearing a safari suit and drinking a gin & tonic in a jungly colonial hotel, the kind with planter chairs and ceiling fans. I found myself thinking that I'd love to turn this fantasy into some sort of reality. I also took comfort in the thought that only a few years before the publication of the guide the world had been in the grip of the 'Spanish Influenza', but had obviously recovered, albeit after the death of as many as 50 million people. In defence of Spain, it was only named after the country as their post-war reporting standards were more relaxed and made the pandemic appear to be concentrated there.

In the days ahead I contemplated the concept of a grand tour on the rails in Thailand a lot more, and each time managed to push the plan slightly further forward. Okay, it might not be possible to travel overseas yet, but I could plan an itinerary, choose the hopping-off points and start to learn about the history of the State Railway of Thailand. I re-sorted my books so that Thailand had its own separate pile on my desk. It wasn't a very big pile. Christian Wolmar wrote a book about the railways that transformed the world called *Blood, Iron & Gold*, but I could only find a single paragraph in it on the Thailand–Burma railway. I had to seek out more niche books. *The Railways of Thailand* by R. Ramaer and *On Track* by Paul Gittins became my new bibles. I followed the usual procedure – post-it notes, coloured pens and maps. You can never have too many maps.

I tried to keep track of what was happening in other parts of the world, and thought of my friends living through bigger waves of infection, some in places with seriously draconian laws. At first, I naively hoped it would soon be over, but of course the reality, as with Spanish Flu, was that there were going to be several waves, and it might take a few years before we got back to what the new normal was going to be. The moment that I had my first vaccination in early 2021 felt like a small miracle, a turning point, and the follow-up dose made me feel like I might now have special powers. The nurse gave me a little vaccination card and put a sticker on me to reinforce my new status. By the time booster doses arrived with a newly tweaked vaccine it felt like we were on the road to normality, but in other parts of the world the approach was still very different.

As the possibility of travel approached I kept a close eye on the rules in place for entering Thailand. They changed most weeks, often with further clarification and more changes after each announcement. Thailand reported Covid cases and deaths each day, rather strangely splitting out foreigners and prisoners from its general population, as if it were trying to pin the blame for transmission of the virus on particular groups. When the borders first reopened anyone wanting to enter the kingdom had to undergo a lengthy quarantine, possibly in a hospital. This was just too tough, but I was ready like a coiled spring for when the rules were relaxed. Eventually a new system was rumoured. It was called the Thailand Pass, all the red tape and new requirements in a semi-friendly wrapper, complete with an online system that delivered unpredictable results to hopeful travellers. Videos started appearing online about how to improve your chances of getting approved and how to work around the application getting rejected for all sorts of crazy administrative reasons. I felt for the people waiting up all night for the email to arrive confirming their fate before their flight the next day. But I'm quite good at red tape, so I was up for it. For the first time the consequences of doing nothing, staying at home for longer, felt worse than taking the risk of catching the dreaded 'rona'[2].

The flight from London to Bangkok was very cheap. Few travellers wanted to take the risk of the health and financial consequences of a Covid holiday. It felt amazing to press the button on the booking – I was finally going to be back out in the world! And so the process of assembling the required documents began. Proof of vaccinations, proof of enhanced medical insurance, proof of reservations at an approved quarantine hotel and an extended-stay visa that required proof of my income and almost everything other than my inside leg measurement. [3] After this there would be last-minute pre-departure testing, on-arrival testing, and Day 5 testing. It was a massive hassle,

[2] a contemporary nickname for the coronavirus

[3] It's 28 inches, in case you were wondering.

but passing the tests would be a gold-plated Willy Wonka ticket to get on with my life.

Disturbing videos began to circulate on the internet about what happened to you if you tested positive for Covid on arrival in Thailand, and there was little information on the process of enforced quarantine. Some were total travel nightmares. I watched one film made by a young European man who gets a knock on the door of his quarantine hotel room whilst awaiting his test result. Outside are a team of medical people in full hazmat suits who take him away to a field hospital, a grim dormitory with poor sanitation and no one who speaks any English. The story gets more bizarre as he manages to escape, is recaptured, and eventually gets moved to a hotel converted into a place for infected foreigners.

No one was officially talking about what benefits the compulsory health insurance provided, or what options you had if you were unlucky enough to test positive. What a disaster that would be for my plans. To counter the risk, I figured that if I had contact with absolutely no one for a couple of weeks before I set off and then had a negative test result just before leaving for the airport, even if I caught Covid on the flight I would be unlikely to test positive on arrival just a few hours later. I had some ideas about the Day 5 test, too, but would face that scenario in due course.

When I booked my flights I didn't worry too much about the departure date – after all, I was going away for a couple of months. This turned out to be a schoolboy error, as I was leaving London the day after a bank holiday weekend. I needed to have proof of a negative PCR test taken less than 72 hours before departure, and most of the laboratories would be closed. No problem I thought, when I booked a drive-through service at a distant football ground with an always-open lab. They emailed me just a few days before I was due to leave telling me that there was, unsurprisingly, a football match on at the weekend, so my appointment was cancelled. I'd never thought that I would end up with the stress of last-minute arrangements, but there it was – I was going to have to get a test the day before my departure. It was in the early hours of the morning I was due to set off that my negative test result finally came through. I breathed a sigh of relief. This was the final piece of paper to put in my red tape folder.

It felt strange to be back at an airport after two years at home. A blend of giddy excitement and a mild fear of mingling with so many people all in one place. I sat in a lounge with passengers wearing masks which they took off to eat and drink as though the virus would not infect you at those moments. All it took was one person to cough, and everyone was on edge. But one of the truisms of travel is that it provides instant escapism from the place that you leave behind. As soon as I found my seat on the plane I just forgot about those two years of lockdown life. What lay ahead was of mild concern, but the inertia and negativity were now out of my head. I was either going to catch it or not catch it, but it was a risk well worth taking to get my adventures back on track.

Bang Sue Junction

Chapter Three
Nana

There is something wonderful about arriving at an Asian airport early in the morning. The rush of humid air when the aircraft opens its doors, the radiation of the sun through the glass of the jet bridge and the smell of musty air conditioning. The sounds of announcements in a language that I don't understand and the beeping noises of weird buggies. Not just the boring ones ferrying wealthy passengers to their first-class lounges, but strange sci-fi-like vehicles transporting cleaners and police around the terminal building.

My head, thick from too much pinot noir and not enough sleep, is jolted by the clarion call that sounds the same in airports throughout the world:

'Caution, end of escalator – caution, end of escalator.' It would be nice to think a real person gets paid royalties for this announcement based on the number of times it gets played, but I think it's the synthesised voice of artificial intelligence. The walkways are so long that you have to decide if it might be worth getting on one even if it carries on past where you want to go, in case it's quicker to go past and then double back on foot. I always admire the passengers that rush past as though they don't want to waste a moment or are hurrying for an impossibly tight connection. All that's missing is a finish line and a medal for completing the distance. But I'm in no real hurry and I am saving my limited energy for the ordeal I have heard about that lies ahead. I wish I had brought along a bag with wheels, but I have chosen something vaguely military, a backpack that is rugged and covered in straps and zips. Wheels are clearly not a combat requirement for this type of luggage.

Bangkok's Suvarnabhumi Airport is both huge and futuristic. Just when you think you are making progress, you discover that you are still walking down a pier that will eventually connect to the main terminal building. The architect who designed the building was definitely a big Star Wars fan. The building looks uncannily like a corridor on the Death Star, but with added retail concessions. Curved thermally insulated windows are wrapped in a dark grey piped exoskeleton. All that's missing are storm troopers and droids. I can see, up front in the distance, masked passengers being gently kettled into a zone filled with a sea of little blue plastic chairs, just like the ones you might have used in a primary school classroom. Officials are dressed in white hazmat suits with full PPE. Welcome to pandemic Thailand.

Waiting to be called forward to a desk I decide to stand, as the chairs are so small that if I were to sit down I may never manage to get back up again. They take the temperatures of batches of travellers in front of trestle tables and then examine their paperwork. I have everything ready in a plastic folder ready for inspection. I even have a back-up folder with duplicate documents in case something should ever get mislaid from the first folder. You might think I'm going too far, but I have a laminating machine in my office at home and I find it pretty hard not to encapsulate important documents in plastic to protect them. I just can't stop myself, in a calming ritual of OCD over-preparation.

My first encounter with the Thai temperature machine is instructive, as I have never come across something like this before. Somewhere between waist and head height a little white box with an all-seeing eye stares at you. Unsure how to interact

Bang Sue Junction

with it, I bend over and look at it close up as though it is a retinal scanner or it might read the temperature of my head. 'Hello, little fella,' I say to it, just in case it has voice capabilities. But a staff member quickly points out the error of my ways – it turns out you just place your palm in front of the sensor. When I move on to the desk my documents are examined, and in receipt of a nod possibly approving my high level of organisation, I am through the first hoop in just a couple of minutes and pointed in the direction of Immigration. There are no longer any big snaking queues here. As I dance the dance of mask and glasses off for photos but back on straight away, my fingerprints are taken and then I hear the satisfying thud of a stamp permitting me to enter the Kingdom of Thailand.

Travel with a mask is not only uncomfortable, it's a barrier to communication in the land of smiles. I'm going to have to learn to use hand signals more. I'm not entirely sure if a thumbs-up sign here is a good thing or a rude gesture. I will consult the internet later.

I have always felt that the worst thing that might happen at the start of any new adventure is to find out that the airline has lost my bag. I normally start to relax when I see my case emerge from the bowels of the terminal and up onto the baggage belt, so I relax when I finally spot it. The only other pre-pandemic ritual is not looking too shifty walking through customs. Today I walk straight through with my best confident, but not so confident that I might look dodgy, mask-covered face. Then out through the sliding frosted glass doors and into arrivals, where I am greeted by total pandemonium. Crowds of jetlagged and confused passengers are trying to find a representative from their official quarantine hotels. Under the rules, the approved hotel has to take you to hospital in a sealed vehicle for testing. There are no taxis or other forms of transport available here today. I find a desk which has a sign indicating that it covers all hotels beginning with the letter L and work my way to the front of the tightly packed scrum. For some reason there is no one here from my hotel. I'm directed to Desk 11, which is concerning as there are no more desks here after Desk 10. I manage to crack the code, though; it's at another exit. There is much milling around and nowhere to socially distance as passengers wait for their hospital-approved minivans. The following day news of this chaos is all over the Bangkok press.

From the back of my van I watch the familiar sight of Bangkok waking up and going to work. The highways are already jammed, and we make random lane changes to save a few feet here and

Bang Sue Junction

there as motorbikes squeeze past at suicidal speed. Things are a little bit different here in the back. There is a Perspex screen sealing me into my own world from the driver. Newly installed plastic ducting provides a fresh air supply to me, and a separate pipe to the driver. He doesn't speak to me, and even if he did I would not be able to hear him, so I just assume he knows how this is going to work. The drill at the hospital turns out to be impressively well organised. It's a drive-through, and my pre-labelled test kit is ready in a plastic basket with its associated paperwork. In the layby awaiting my arrival are a team of medical staff who check my passport to make sure I'm the same person as the one in their documentation. I have heard about how in some countries it's standard procedure to push the PCR swab so far up your nose that you feel like you have just had brain surgery, but I need not have worried today, as the nurse is very gentle with me. All done and I'm off to quarantine at a nearby approved hotel.

I have always enjoyed getting into a nice hotel room after a lengthy journey. A chance to wash off the grime of travel and relax in a private cocoon of comfort. But today I'm in a nice room with a twist – I can't leave. It's my very own luxury prison cell. I'm showered and changed into fresh clothes by 7am local time, but with absolutely nowhere to go. I have a telephone for room service, and a minibar with a few cans of beer. On the wall is a big television, with channels of Thai news that I can't understand. There is a huge bed with the kind of sheets that you only find in expensive hotels. I find myself pacing up and down the room measuring my steps; I have seen too many prison movies. At one end of my room – fourteen steps – I pause by the door to look out of the spyhole at an empty corridor. No one is there to take me away, at least not yet. Will they call up to my room first to let me know the results, or try to take me by surprise at the door? My imagination is getting the better of me. I think that if they sent me off to a field hospital I would need therapy for life, and I cannot afford to lose ten days of my travel plan. I keep reminding myself that it is pretty unlikely that I am going to test positive, but I have constructed a conspiracy theory in my head that the hotels and hospitals are in collusion to reap the rewards of my expensive medical insurance.

I always unpack, even if I'm only staying somewhere for a day or two. I even unpack on trains sometimes. On the desk I lay out my paperwork, a variety of chargers, a jungle of USB cables and a range of devices that mostly require different connections. In prison films I always admire the inmates who better themselves by studying to make use of all that empty time. Settling down at the desk and with nothing better to usefully do, I open my map of the Thai rail network. This adventure isn't going to be an A to B kind of journey. The railway lines radiate outward from Bangkok to near and far provinces. There are four main lines – the Northern Line up to Chiang Mai, the Southern Line down to Hat Yai and on to Malaysia, the Eastern Line down to Rayong and also over to the Cambodian border at Aranyaprathet, and the Northeastern Line to Ubon Ratchathani and the Lao border at Nong Khai in the far east of the country – and each main line has branch lines.

Every railway has its own distinctive ways of working, and I'll have to get the hang of the State Railway of Thailand (SRT). It runs trains with at least three different classes, plus day trains, sleeper trains, air-conditioned trains and even some with open windows and fans. The rolling stock is a mixture of Chinese, Japanese, Korean and Thai-built carriages. You can travel in anything from a private room in an ultra-modern air-conditioned sleeper through to a simple wooden bench seat in a third-class carriage. This is going to be a deep dive into life on the rails in Thailand. I have already made reservations for a couple of journeys that get booked up; a local travel agent bought them for me the moment they went on sale. But some other tickets are only available on the day before departure.

Nana

I have much to learn if I am to master the system. Once I am released from quarantine, though, my first trip will be easy to arrange: a journey up to Nam Tok, as far as the line extends towards Myanmar on a branch of the Southern Line. Apparently I can just turn up and buy a ticket on the day, as it is a third-class Ordinary train.

After a few more sessions pacing around the room and with no sign of imminent detention, I sit down on the edge of my bed. Jetlag is kicking in, a force that's hard to fight when you travel east. You have to straddle both time zones and then push through to avoid spending the day in bed and becoming a creature of the night. I decide to allow myself a quick snooze, but as soon as my head touches the pillow I drift into a strange sleep, the sort where you are semi-conscious yet unable to wake up or move. When I finally open my eyes I can immediately tell it's much later in the day as the sun has moved round to the other side of the room. Where am I? After a moment's thought, Bangkok, yes, I'm in a Bangkok hotel bedroom. I gradually tune back into my surroundings. Other than the hum of the air conditioning I realise I have been woken by the phone, which has a ring tone from the 1980s. I find the vintage device on the bedside table. It's the kind with a flashing red light and buttons to call all sorts of hotel services that are probably not available to people like me in quarantine. When I lift the receiver, I forget to say anything. 'Mr Matthew?' a friendly female voice asks. 'We have your result. You test negative.'

Although I had thought it would be unlikely I would test positive, it is still a relief to have it officially confirmed. The nightmare of the field hospital is now behind me. 'You mean I can leave now, I mean, go outside?' What a stupid thing to ask, but the news is exhilarating. A whole country to explore and rediscover without too much more red tape.

'Yes, you can go. We have a le'er from the hospital here at front desk,' she says in an excited tone. I thank her and put the phone down. I'm quite a repressed person, and I can't manage a whoop or a holler. Instead I just punch the air with my fists and smile. It's time to get out and organise my first trip on the rails.

In the manner of a recently released convict reacclimatising to life, I stroll out of the hotel with a tingling sense of anticipation of the world outside the thick plate-glass doors. The streets look different to how I remember them, but it's far from being the ghost town that I've heard about in the middle of the pandemic. I am staying in a district of town that most people know for its preponderance of rather seedy bars. The hotel is respectable enough, but nearby is Nana Plaza, a flagship multistorey mecca for Thailand's brand of adult entertainment. The stereotype of ageing Western men with financially compensated companionship is everywhere around me. I wish I had some sort of badge declaring myself not a sex tourist. If only people knew that I'm really an undercover rail enthusiast.

I am in fact only a few feet away from my first rail journey of the trip. Named after the similar system that runs in Vancouver, the BTS[4] Skytrain first opened in 1999, offering a futuristic way to speed over the top of the gridlocked roads beneath. I love elevated trains, and Bangkok now has more than 70 km of raised tracks on three lines carving through the middle of the city. There are already over sixty stations with several privately financed extensions planned. I don't think the Blade Runner films had any elevated trains, but in the absence of flying cars this is the way to get around a modern city.

As soon as you step onto the escalator up to the first level of the station you are removed from the hustle and bustle, but you can still observe street life from above. After buying a Rabbit card, I make my way up to the next level, a simple split of a

---

[4] Bangkok Transit System

platform in each direction. Integrated transport payment cards are great, but unfortunately in Bangkok this card only works on the BTS, so you need to pay for express boat trips and MRT[5] trains by cash or another card. I imagine contactless debit card payments will leap ahead and be used for all forms of transport before too long. The doors of my train slide shut and we draw smoothly out of Nana Station. I look into the windows of the nearby offices as we pass by and I wonder what the people behind their desks are working on. I'd like to have struck up a conversation with fellow passengers, but strangely one of the current rules – in addition to no water pistols or durian fruit – is no talking.

When I enter the refrigerated environment of a shopping mall a couple of stops away I have to go through the temperature check again. I throw the machine a low five, and the guard waves me in. As I pass him I slaver my hands in the antibacterial gel provided, hoping to gain extra merit. Locals escape the outside world in buildings like this. It's a grand day out with places to shop, eat and watch a movie without knowing what the time of day is, or what the weather is doing outside. You can probably

---

[5] Metropolitan/Mass Rapid Transit

guess about the weather, though, as it will be mostly hot, and then repeatedly hot and wet.

Asian malls nearly always have the same layout, and in the basement I find an ATM and a supermarket where I can pick up supplies for my first trip. I max out on instant noodles and crisps with exotic-sounding flavours. I hope they live up to the pictures, as I have never sampled chilli squid or Hat Yai chicken flavour chips before. There must be Thai people arriving in London who are equally fascinated by prawn cocktail or sausage and tomato flavours.

On my way back to the hotel I come across a shifty man selling an extensive range of oversized and brightly coloured sex toys in the shadows of a footbridge. I pretend not to notice him and he doesn't hassle me. Unfortunately, in avoiding him I manage to walk straight into the arms of a lady boy, who grabs me by the arm. 'Hello, lovely man. Where you going?' she – or is it he? – asks. I'm not sure what the right protocols are. Dressed as she is in a black leather skirt, a leopard-skin bodice and 6-inch heels, I can see how some men get distracted and fail to spot the tell-tale sign of an Adam's apple. Sensing I might not be interested in her idea of a fun night out, she pulls out all the stops. Just as I'm wriggling free of her grasp she flutters her eyelashes and says, 'Why are you so cute?'

Help! Slipping backwards, I duck under a sign and quickly climb the stairs of an overpass. On the other side of the busy street I spot an unusual-looking shop. It has strange bird symbols painted above the door, and a sign beneath – Almas Barber. I badly need a haircut. In an attempt to avoid catching pre-travel Covid back at home I also avoided the risks of a short back and sides for more than two months on the basis that hairdressers were a place where catching the virus was a certainty. Almas looks like it might be the go-to place to get a haircut in Nana, so I open the door and step inside.

The man who greets me isn't built like a typical Thai man; he's maybe 5' 5", chunky but strong with close-cropped hair and a glint in his eye. He isn't wearing a mask, and his wide smile reveals some expensive gold dentistry. He introduces himself as Aki. He's an Iranian citizen who managed to survive being shot twice and then gassed in the Iraq–Iran war before making his escape to Europe. Thirty-something years later he is now a demon Bangkok barber, and a man who owns no less than 1200 ducks at a farm near Hat Yai. Aki isn't cutting hair today – he explains that he's too tired – but he supervises a young man who takes careful measurements of my head before proceeding with the timid precision of someone who might not have cut much hair before. The only word I understand from the master's instructions is '*nid noi*' – just a little.

Chatting with Aki provides a useful distraction from the progress of my haircut. I get a detailed insight into life in Iran, and the Iran–Iraq war. 'You need to hit the head of the snake,' he tells me. I try to memorise his pearls of wisdom in case they might come in useful on my travels. Handing me his business card, he tells me that he has brothers all over Thailand and can sort out any problems that I might encounter. I thank him, tip his apprentice and leave. Glancing at myself in the mirror by the doorway, I see I have moved on from 1970s rock drummer. I am now sporting a hairstyle rather similar to the lead singer of 1980s English futurist group A Flock of Seagulls.

Back at the empty reception of my hotel, I stop by the front desk to collect my proof of test result. It's presented to me in the style of a school swimming certificate, except that you don't get a badge to sew onto your trunks. If the staff were not behind their protective plastic screen they probably would have arranged a selfie. I'm encouraged to keep it with me at all times in the envelope provided – another bit of red tape for my folder.

It's the early evening here, but the GMT hand on my watch reminds me that it's only lunchtime back in the UK. The bar outside the hotel has draught beer on a happy hour promotion, and I'm not one to miss the chance of a free beer. Ingesting the fumes of traffic combined with the contents of a frosted glass, I do my best to bat off the flies feasting on my exposed ankles. Their bites are savage, and I start to bleed in a few places, but I decide that this is a small price to pay for my freedom.

I could spend the evening here, but I need to pack for tomorrow's journey, so I return to my now open cell on the 14th floor. From the safe distance of my vantage point up here I can see the brightly coloured lights of the entertainment district of Nana down below. I put my bag on the bed and lay my gear out. My 1928 *Guide to Bangkok* suggests 'light summer clothing used in England with the addition of a sun hat will answer the requirements'. I'm going to travel light for the first trip, so I follow the well-versed advice of halving the amount of stuff I put out at first. That does not seem to work, so I halve it again, which is probably about right. Then I put everything I'm not taking into my suitcase, which I will leave in store here until I return.

Going to bed is more challenging than I'd expected it to be. I can't work out how to turn all the lights out. When I turn the bedside lights out the ones in the room remain on. Back out of bed, I turn those off and repeat. This time the desk lights stubbornly remain on. Then when I have dealt with those, the lamp by the window comes on. At this I give up; too embarrassed to call down to reception, I remove the offending light bulbs. I drift into a Chang-induced[6] sleep and dream the happy dreams of someone who is about to set out on an adventure that had seemed impossible only a few months ago.

---

[6] Chang is one of the biggest domestic beer brands in Thailand

Bang Sue Junction

Chapter Four
Man on Fire

After a long shower and a reasonable socially distanced breakfast buffet, I set off to Thonburi Station on the other side of the Chao Phraya River. I have to be back in Bangkok for another PCR test in three days' time, so my plan is to take the relatively short trip up to the north west, to Nam Tok. Rather confusingly, it's the Southern Line that I will be taking, but before it turns south a branch splits off, taking a route towards the border with Myanmar. Many travellers still know this line as the Death Railway.

The temperature inside the cab is set at 24°C. I'm a well-known grumbler when it comes to hot taxis,

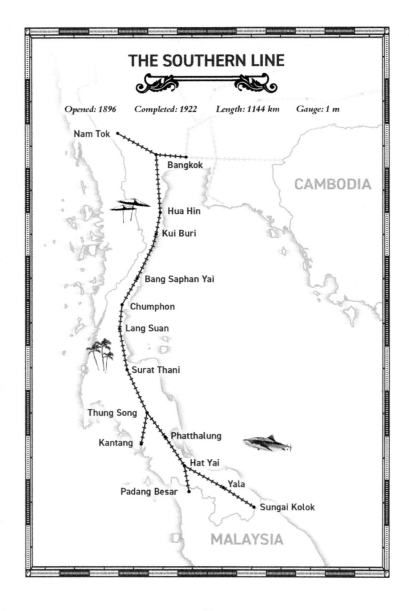

but today this feels like an ice box compared to the temperature outside, even though it is only 6am. As in many cabs in Asia, this one's windscreen is festooned with mobile devices and has cameras pointing in all directions. The car has some custom go-faster accessories too: a large rubberised steering wheel cover for better grip and an aluminium gear knob for slicker shifts. My driver weaves along Sukhumvit Road, using mainly second and third gears for optimum torque when he needs to switch lanes. Just as I'm beginning to get used to the pace we have a minor collision with a tuk tuk, [7] which according to my driver's gesticulations is definitely not our fault. No details are formally exchanged, just sharp words that I don't understand. Then we carry on. I'm pleased that I have my seatbelt on. When I ask my driver to slow down he looks at me pityingly in the rear-view mirror. 'No – *no* go slow,' he tells me, as though to reduce speed would be against his street racing values. It's not lost on me that we are on the same road where James Bond raced his stolen AMC Hornet in pursuit of Scaramanga in *The Man with the Golden Gun*. I'm relieved when we finally pull up outside the station. I expect to pay close change – that is, until the traffic behind us gets restless. It's too early in the morning to argue.

---

[7] an auto-rickshaw or motor-scooter cab

I grab my bag, pull it over my shoulders and step up into the open-air station concourse.

Bangkok Noi Station first opened in 1903. It used to be the main terminus of the Southern Line, with its buffers right on the banks of the Chao Phraya River. But, bombed by the Americans during the Second World War, it has been rebuilt, and even relocated a couple of times. Its 'temporary' site at Thonburi, further back from the river, has now become, for the time being at least, its permanent location.

This morning I'm taking Train 257 up to the other end of a branch of the line to Nam Tok, just under 125 miles (201 km) away. I peer through the window in the ticket office, behind which sits a man with an old computer that has turned yellow in the sun. He has a lot of medals, his left breast boasting two rows of neatly sewn ribbons. I ask him for a return ticket, but back only as far as the station at the River Khwae bridge. If you have not heard of the Khwae before you might have thought this was a typo. In fact, the waterway made famous by David Lean's 1957 film about the bridge was actually the Mae Klong River, but in 1960, in order to tie fact and fiction together, it had its name changed. It was renamed the Khwae Yai. 'Khwae' is easily mispronounced 'Kwai' by non-Thai-speaking people, and with the success of the film this allowed visitors to relate to the river as the Kwai or Khwae.

'Passport,' he says without looking up. Really? A passport for this train? I'm not planning on going to Myanmar. I slide it across to him through a little slot in the window, and he taps my name and number into the computer. 'You pay 100 baht.' I ask him how much for the return to the bridge, just 50 miles (80 km), and he says, 'Also 100 baht, buy at Nam Tok.' In fact, any journey, however short or long, on this line costs 100 baht to a foreigner. I find out later that locals pay just 39 baht for the same journey. This dual pricing system may not sound very fair on the face of it, but as the five-hour journey is costing me about £2.50 I'm not going to argue.

He passes back my passport together with a small white paper ticket. I have no seat reservation, as it's a free-for-all in 'Class 3 seating coach (fan)'. The date is at first confusing, as the Thai Buddhist-era calendar is 543 years ahead of the Gregorian one that I'm used to, but I'm reassured by another passenger that my ticket is for today's train. The ticket machine can print in English as well as Thai, and it does the conversion from one to the other, presumably because I haven't produced Thai ID. The assumption is that I can't read Thai. I wonder if Cambodian or Laotian travellers might prefer

Thai to English, but it's academic at the moment, as the borders are closed.

The first thing I notice on the platform is the well-turned-out stationmaster. The SRT must have its own version of Sandhurst, where much attention is paid to turnout and deportment. The sun is low but rising, and everything is washed in a golden glow. I badly need a coffee, but there is none for sale here, so I settle for a Sprite, served to me in a plastic bag with a straw. I find a seat next to a happy monk and wait for our train. The monk seems so happy that I consider if he might actually be a drunk monk. Someone told me that there are a few fake monks around, who are really beggars in disguise. I don't know if that's true or not. How do you tell? I don't think monks carry official monk ID.

There are only a handful of tourists waiting here today for a train that would once have been full of travellers headed to the bridge or to hike in the jungle and see the elephants. But there are still some great travel clichés around me. A couple of European girls with bandanas are playing cards, which seems to fascinate the Thai men, and a loved-up American couple are taking it in turns to strum tunes on a small guitar.

At about 7.15am a diesel locomotive pulls up on the opposite platform. It's a refurbished 1960s General Electric, with its distinctive scooped yellow front end. It is hauling the 255 Ordinary train bound for Lang Suan, down the coast past Hua Hin. A handful of passengers climb on, and the stationmaster gives the signal on his bell, freeing the train to grumble off down the line.

If you had a train set as a kid you'd feel right at home here at Thonburi. The carriages, which are kept in sidings behind the station, need to be shunted out and attached to an engine. There is no turntable, so the locomotives use the sidings to detach them, then re-attach at the right end of the train. The slight complication is that the sidings are not deep enough to take all the carriages, making shunting impossible if a train is already in the station. It's a classic Hornby starter layout.

With Train 255 out of the way our locomotive now arrives at our platform. It doesn't have any carriages yet, but this is a promising start. A second engine then shunts some pretty battered carriages around and onto the same track. The guard shouts at people, telling them to stay on the platform, but he's mostly ignored. The reason for his shouts becomes clear as the carriages are coupled to the locomotive with a violent shunt, throwing two people off the steps of the first carriage and back onto the platform. Fortunately, no one is hurt. He did warn people – why didn't they listen to him? This is my first lesson on the Thai approach to health and safety. There isn't really such a thing. That's why so many people die on the roads, and – fortunately to a much lesser degree – on the rails too. Train tracks are not seen as dangerous places, but as helpful aids to walking, setting up a barbecue or a shortcut crossing when driving home from work.

There is something cultural going on here. I grew up in England in the 1970s. The government was keen that kids should not go anywhere near the tracks, so the British Railways Board commissioned several graphic and quite disturbing films to highlight the perils of playing on railway lines. Today the films might be rated with an 18 certificate, but those were different times, and they were shown in primary schools. The first one, in 1977 was called *The Finishing Line*. It somehow combined a school sports day with being killed on the railway. It was pretty chilling stuff. But the one I remember the most was called *Robbie,* released in 1979. It is the story of a sweet eight-year-old football-mad boy who is encouraged by his brother to trespass on the railway tracks. He meets with several different accidents, as they made different versions of the film for ordinary tracks, overhead electric, and electric third rail. In one version he is electrocuted, and in another has both his feet amputated. Robbie is then in a wheelchair and can play football no more.

Thailand has its own way of communicating rail safety: illustrated posters. The scenes are gruesome, but a man losing his head with blood spurting everywhere looks more like a cartoon than a real-life scenario. Somehow these posters don't scare me in the same way as the British films did. But I think that the main difference to attitude is cultural: Thai people are brought up to take chances and will get away with whatever they can as a way of life – quite different to the traditionally British way of doing what we are told without question, even if with a bunch of grumbles.

I'm brought back to the here and now by the whistle of the train guard. He follows this with an arm signal that I assume means it is now safe for us to get on board the train. He looks down the line of now obedient passengers, and smiles, appreciative of us waiting for his permission. The carriages all look to be in pretty similar condition, so I choose one towards the rear of the train. Some third-class coaches have plastic-covered bench seats, others just painted wood. All have invitingly open windows. The outside of my carriage today is painted in the SRT's current yellow, cream and plum colours. Ceiling fans whir about, and people find the best seats they can in the shade. I always sit where the locals do. Last time I took a train like this I sat on the sunny side and got a sunburnt arm. Big mistake. I used to think that the metal shutters were some form of security to stop people throwing things into or out of the train. In fact, they are ventilated grilles that provide protection from the sun but still allow a slight breeze into the coach. Settling into a plastic seat in the shade, I push the counter-weighted window down in the frame as far as it will go. The guard passes through, helping other people do the same. The carriage is not too full, just a nice place to relax and watch the world go by the window.

Three dings, the distinctive General Electric grumble, and we're off, jittering and swaying along the line. The forward motion creates a breeze through the windows on each side of the coach, and if you don't mind breathing in the mix of air, dust and exotic smells it's quite pleasant. It is currently compulsory to wear a mask in a public place in Thailand, and I think I have finally found one of the few occasions when a mask is actually a good idea.

You know when the ticket inspectors are approaching without having to look up. They don't even need to ask for tickets, they just click their ticket punches. It's a very distinctive sound: metal on metal, like miniature walnut crackers without the nuts to worry about. Close behind them is a happy brigade of food sellers offering cooked breakfast, sweet snacks and cold drinks from their baskets.

The tracks pass just a few feet from rows of wooden shacks with corrugated iron roofs. At first I think of this as a shanty town, but maybe it isn't. There are little houses with electricity and satellite TV. Animals graze on their land and kids swim in the nearby khlongs,[8] presumably before going to school. There are also a lot of new-looking scooters and bikes parked nearby. I wonder what the residents do for a living. By night a simple life on the edge of the rails, yet perhaps working in city office jobs during the day?

As we weave through the urban jungle, our driver sounds the horn as we approach road crossings. Vehicles regularly get taken out by trains in Thailand at its many unmanned and sometimes unofficial crossings. Between the road junctions we make a number of quick stops. A squeal of brakes, red flag, three dings, green flag and we're off again in about 30 seconds. The carriage gradually fills up with passengers, especially when we stop at the city of Nakhon Pathom, about 30 miles (48 km) west

---

[8] canals

of Bangkok. The passengers sitting around me are mainly family groups and schoolkids, and a sprinkling of foreign travellers. There is a nice atmosphere, with people talking to each other and munching on various freshly delivered snacks.

The landscape opens out to reveal plains of pineapple and mango plantations and fields of almost ripe corn. Storks nest on the telegraph poles, and alongside the track water buffalo eat the sparse green vegetation on the embankment, charred and black from a recent fire. When we pass sections that are still ablaze, the pungent smoke is sucked into the carriage. This is slash and burn, the clearing and fertilising of the land with ash before the oncoming rainy season.

When I'm not staring out of the window I'm reading an account of a prisoner of war who survived the Death Railway. I'm full of that feeling of sense of place. It's a strange sensation. I put my book down as I'm having problems reading – and it's not my eyesight that's causing this. People around me are starting to cough, and this is not Covid. Smoke is drifting around us, and ash is swirling in from both sides of the carriage. Then a thick blanket of smoke engulfs us, creating a total whiteout. I manage to remain calm until I smell singed hair, and then realise I might need to do something. My eyes stream with tears before I have to close them. I'm not sure why, but I decide to adopt the aircraft brace position, something I'm pleased to say that I have never actually had to do on a plane. Maybe there will be less smoke down nearer the floor. Brushing the smouldering grass out of my hair, I do my best to breathe normally. I don't know how long this lasts for, but when I open my eyes again I still can't see anything much at all – inside the carriage is just a haze. But it is clearing. I take off my glasses and wipe my eyes. Everything looks normal, and some passengers seem remarkably unfazed by the experience. I see a monk a few rows in front of me wipe the ash from his sweating shaven head. He's clearly made of tough stuff. He probably does a fire walk on burning coals before breakfast each day. I hope his robes are made of a non-flammable material. Thankful that I have not actually caught fire, I get out some wet wipes and clean up my sweaty skin as best as I can. The guard wanders through a few minutes later and acts as though nothing out of the ordinary has happened.

When the train pulls into Kanchanaburi quite a few people get off the train, leaving more space for the remaining passengers to spread out beside the windows. It's after a brief stop at Wang Pho Station that I realise that I'm now sitting on the wrong side. Not because of the sun or the shade, but because on my side all I can see is a rock face close up, whereas on the other side there is an impressive view of the drop down to the river below. The train appears to be in the air, supported by a rickety 400-metre trestle bridge attached to the cliff face. Tourists are actually standing on the bridge, and as our train creeps past they huddle into enclaves off the track. This is an amazing location to take pictures of yourself and your friends about to be run over by a train, but only as long as you have not already fallen through the tracks and into the river far below. In a very Thai way, this is a perfect tourist attraction. A place to have lunch, walk the railway line, visit a temple in a cave, take photographs, buy souvenirs and then return to Bangkok by train, all in a day. But I wonder how many of these day trippers know about the dark past of this viaduct, the Tham Kra Sae Bridge. It was originally built by 2000 prisoners of war and forced labourers in an incredible seventeen days in April 1943, and is one of the more distinctive remaining features of the Siam–Burma railway. A number of prisoners were killed when explosives were used to blow holes in the cliff face, and many more lost their footing and fell to their death into the ravine beneath.

When we head further north, I've pretty much got the carriage to myself. Then, as we part company with the riverside, the train gains speed, heading across the plains. In the distance I can see mountains that are probably in Myanmar. Neat piles of dried and unfamiliar crops line the fields. As we bank and bounce around shallow curves, no matter how I stow it, my water bottle rolls onto the floor and from side to side of the carriage. Then the train slows, and with a few blasts on the horn the driver pulls us gently into Nam Tok. In just 5 hours I have reached my first end-of-the-line objective. Technically it isn't, though, as at the weekend a tourist train travels slightly further on, to some waterfalls at nearby Nam Tok Sai Yok Noi. But my regular train can't go any further, as there is no room up there for its diesel locomotive to shunt around the carriages for the return journey, but the weekend train is a multiple-unit which can travel in either direction.

The tracks from here used to continue onwards to Hellfire Pass and they eventually crossed into Burma, but after the end of the war part of the line at the border was removed and the rest of the line north of Nam Tok reverted to jungle. The Myanmar border is 177 miles (285 km) away on the route of the original railway. It would be nice to think that one day there will be a cross-border connection again, but rebuilding the railway is not going to be straightforward. The area is surrounded by mountains, and part of the route has been flooded by a reservoir.

I briefly consider an Indiana Jones escapade into the jungle. I might be able to follow the route of the tracks, befriend the hill tribes and sneak into Burma overland. 'Briefly' means for about five seconds; I can barely handle the heat here in the shade of the station platform and I can't imagine what it must be like in the sweltering jungle. Do they still have tigers? Fortunately, I have no compass or machete in my bag today, just a packed lunch and a copy of the Royal State Railways of Siam 1928 *Guide to Bangkok*.

Hellfire Pass, the restored Death Railway cutting, is an easy songthaew[9] ride from the railway station. From such a dark past, the place has become totally peaceful and well maintained. I'd like to spend longer here, but need to get back to Kanchanaburi on the afternoon train.

---

[9] a shared taxi service in a pickup truck

Chapter Five
Bridge on the River Kwai

The journey back from Nam Tok on Train 233 is uneventful. We don't catch fire even once. The station office at Nam Tok is closed, so I buy a ticket from the guard on the train. No passport is required, but I still don't get the local price; it costs me another 100 baht. I sit back and enjoy the scenery as best I can. I'm a little envious of the carefree happiness of the tourists heading home. My mood is contrastingly dark, and I think the underlying reason for this is that I have become dehydrated, which always makes my thinking less rational. I need to take on a couple of litres of water, but that isn't going to happen until we reach the bridge back at Kanchanaburi. My senses are intensified by my condition – the colours outside the carriage are saturated, and the constant tooting of the train's horn is right between my ears.

When we pull into Kwai Bridge Station I clamber down the steps onto the low platform. No one else seems to be getting off here, and that's part of my plan. This is the last train of the day that goes all the way back to Thonburi; perfect for me to explore the bridge after the crowds have left for the day. What I have forgotten, though, is that most visitors arrive here on a tour bus. I'm met by a couple of friendly tourist police at the end of the platform, just in front of the infamous bridge. It's obvious that their main job is to keep people from being run over as they pose for selfies in front of the trains. I find tourist police to be an interesting concept. Without doubt they are very helpful here in Thailand, where things are not always as they seem and cultural misunderstandings can lead to more serious consequences. We have a quick chat about my plans and they point me in the direction of somewhere to stay, handing me a photocopy of a timetable adapted to show all the trains passing through just this station. Online research is great, but an analogue chat with someone on the spot is always reassuring, particularly as the timetables have changed quite a bit during the pandemic. This is known by some as 'ground truth'.

The extent of my dehydration doesn't become clear until I try to walk down the platform in a straight line. I feel a bit dizzy – drunk, even. Instead of sitting in the shade and getting some water on board, irrationally I bite the bullet and hike off in the direction of my accommodation with a rucksack on my back and still wearing sandals. Mad dogs and Englishmen. I need to stop looking at the weather on my phone. Today it helpfully tells me that when factoring in the relative humidity the 38°C temperature here feels like 47°C. 'Feels like' is a mini-science lesson in relative humidity; the amount of moisture the air can hold is greater when it's hotter, thus making the evaporative effect of sweat less efficient. My clothes are quickly soaked with fresh sweat, and my wet t-shirt sticks against my skin. Several locals sitting in the shade ask me where I'm going but I ignore them as I think they might be out to scam me. This is of course heat exhaustion paranoia, and later I wish I'd gone back and apologised as I suspect they were just trying to help.

When I find the place that I am going to stay at I'm not looking at my best. Reception is busy with well-dressed Japanese tourists who have just got out of an air-conditioned minivan. I stand out like a sore thumb here. A young man runs towards me to relieve me of my rucksack and steers me to a seat next to the desk. Once the formalities are complete, I head off to my room, somewhere in a complex of buildings near the banks of the river. But I can't seem to follow the instructions they gave me and I'm quickly lost. My brain has become dysfunctional. I manage to retrace my steps back to reception and the staff arrange an escort.

Once inside my bedroom I pull the curtains closed and step out of my wet clothes, leaving them in a sopping pile by the door. The bathroom is one of those trendy indoor-outdoor places complete with lots of granite and cobbles. I learn to master the controls of the rain shower and gradually return my core temperature to something approaching normal under the heavy jets of cold water. In the darkness of the room I locate a couple of bottles of water, mix in some rehydration sachets and gulp them down before passing out on the bed and letting the sweltering heat of the afternoon pass by. Later on, feeling much better, I dig out some fresh clothes from my bag. I've been told that people who explore jungles have two sets of clothing: a day set that will always be wet, and a dry set for the end of the day and sleeping. In the morning it's back on with the wet set.

Outside it's cooler now, and I find my way to a table right on the bank of the river, from where I can watch the world go by. The sun sinks behind the hills, leaving a moody dusk sky. Just me, with the barman and the cicadas for company. That is until I hear the sound of disco music in the distance. It has a pounding techno beat combined with unfamiliar vocals, and it's getting louder. Then the source of the party swings into view downstream. A floating nightclub packed with people dancing, shouting and drinking beer out of cans. The boat, which has seen better days, is made of wood with a straw canopy above an improvised dance floor. Against the current the boat makes slow progress, so for the next half an hour I'm in the disco, if not actually on the dancefloor. I'm almost close enough to ask the DJ if he has any Spandau Ballet. The boat makes it up river as far as the bridge, then the skipper turns the boat around and it heads back where it came from, now with the current in its favour to help speed it away. Peace is finally restored – on my part of the river, at least.

The following morning the light through the thin curtains wakes me early. I have slept solidly for 8 hours and apart from a slight headache I'm feeling considerably better. Time to explore. The bridge that crosses the river today is one of two that were built during the Second World War. The remains of the original wooden bridge, Number 277, are still visible on the riverbank. Both were bombed and repaired several times during the war. If you examine the remaining bridge you can see not only the original curved steel spans but also two truss sections from Japan that were fitted after the war had ended.

I'm a great fan of David Lean's multi academy award-winning 1957 film, but it is a work of complete fiction. In the film Alec Guinness plays the part of Colonel Nicholson, a character who is so proud of the impressive bridge that his men have built that he wants to protect it. In reality, Lieutenant Colonel Toosey did all he could to sabotage the construction of the bridge, using everything from termites to poorly mixed concrete. Guinness wasn't the first choice for the role, and spent much time arguing with Lean over how to play the character. Lean told him to 'fuck off home' after his filmed parts were complete.

I take a seat on a bench near the bridge and sip on an iced soda whilst listening to a man next to me play 'Imagine' on a beaten-up violin. It fits in rather well, and I guess he knows this. I suspect that over time he has adjusted his playlist to optimise revenue. Pretty much everything is commercialised here. What really alarms me is that across the river I can see a themed restaurant park called Prisoner of War Camp, complete with wire fences, huts and a fake helicopter from the 1960s ... as Major Clipton, the medical officer, says in the film, 'Madness, madness!' The word is that one day this could be the location of a brand new railway hotel. Who knows, perhaps you will be able to stay in the Colonel Toosey Suite, complete with a matchstick model of the original bridge.

Back at the bridge railway station everything is happening at a sedate pace under the shade of improvised tarpaulins. Even the station dogs are sticking to the shade. I spot an old steam train across the track behind the station. This is Locomotive 719, a Japanese engine built in the 1930s. I can't find much about its history, but I imagine it puffing across the bridge with Allied bombers trying to take it out. I'm carrying a list of all the steam trains in Thailand in my bag, and I cross 719 off it. Just seventy-five more to go — and five of them are still running.

Halfway down the platform I meet a lady called Dao selling an impressive selection of hats on her stall. She ushers me into her patch of shade and offers me a seat and some water. I'm touched by her kindness. This isn't a hustle to make me buy something, just someone being friendly. Together we watch day trippers doing crazy things on the tracks, trying to outdo each other to get the perfect Insta picture of the advancing train on the bridge. I remember the Thai word for 'crazy', taught to me by a German hotel manager who had seen a lot of

Bang Sue Junction

it over the years. *'Ba ba baw baw'* I tell her with a nonchalant nod, which makes her grin a betel nut smile. 'You speak Thai!' *'Nid noi'* I tell her – 'Just a little bit'. But a little bit of Thai goes a long way. Just to emphasise the craziness at this moment a man standing in front of us decides to cross the track to the other platform. There is only one track here, and you can board the train from either side. He's had ages to think about crossing, but for some reason has put this off until Train 258 Ordinary is just a few feet away from us. My heart almost stops. Is it that he likes the thrill of a near-death experience? Or that he thinks he is showing off with his blasé attitude to risk?

I say goodbye to my new friend and walk down the platform towards the back of the train. The carriages are not very full, and I find one which has the winning combination of working fans, open windows and padded plastic seats. These third-class Ordinary trains are the backbone of travel between small settlements in the provinces. I don't know why, but in the rail fan community the German expression *fenster auf* gets used a lot to describe the pleasure of an open window. It's an increasingly hard thing to find in our largely air-conditioned world. Today I'm at peak *fenster auf.*

I'm getting used to the importance of the station bell. It's not the Enigma code, but unless you travel

Bridge on the River Kwai

on the rails in Thailand a lot you might not be aware of the language of its rings. Perhaps the single most important signal is the slow three-ding one, which means that the train will depart in one minute. Then it gets slightly more complicated. There is a series of dings, odd and even numbers of dings, depending on whether the train is travelling up or down the line. These communicate that the approaching train is either one or two stops away. Timing is everything, with pauses of different lengths between two dings and a ding-ding. I much prefer this to pre-recorded station announcements. Today the stationmaster's zen ringing style sounds even slower than usual, with a brief meditational period between each ding signalling our imminent departure.

The journey back to Bangkok is slow, and I use the time to follow as much as I can of what I see going on at the stations that we stop at, trying to pick up as much as possible of the rail procedures and general station etiquette. Travelling in this direction, we have to wait a lot more for the oncoming freight trains to pass than we did when going the other way. This is my introduction to the time-honoured system of the token. With only a single track in a number of places, to avoid the possibility of a collision, the driver of the train on that section of the track carries a special coin, or token, in a holster attached to a big hoop. At the station this can be collected on a pole close to the tracks, or just handed down to the stationmaster, who can then give it to the train waiting to travel on the same part of the line in the opposite direction. The drivers cannot proceed without the token in their possession. Rudimentary, but effective.

Some of our stops this afternoon are as long as 20 minutes, and without the dusty breeze of forward momentum the carriages become uncomfortably hot. The closer we get to Bangkok the more the carriage fills up with the mix of passengers you find on pretty much any train in Thailand. There are no distinctions of dress or uniform in the way that can define passengers in Europe. Here young and old, pale and suntanned skin, groups and solo travellers are all jumbled together. A well-behaved group of teenage boys find seats around me. You might find this a bit alarming in some parts of the world, but here there is a relaxed, safe, and happy atmosphere. I decide to break out my jelly baby rations and share them around.

I don't believe many Thai people have come across them before. 'Jelly babies,' I tell them. 'Would you like one?' My words are greeted with something between confusion and mild concern. I try to always carry a bag of Maynard Bassetts'

Bridge on the River Kwai

most famous sweets when I travel – not to eat myself, but more to use as an ice-breaker. Bassetts have been making them since the end of the First World War, when they were actually known as Peace Babies. But my love of them comes from more recent times. Doctor Who first hit British television screens in 1963. As with James Bond, you like the one you grew up with the most, so my Bond was Roger Moore and my Doctor was Tom Baker. You could argue that Sean Connery was the better Bond, or Patrick Troughton was the better Doctor, but these were my actors.

Back in 1974, the Doctor regenerated for the fourth time and Tom Baker arrived, a man who changed my childhood. Instantly recognisable by his long scarf and floppy hat, he was my hero. He was by my side in good times and bad ones. My Time Lord always carried jelly babies in the pocket of his big coat, offering them to extra-terrestrials as a gesture of galactic peace and friendship. This is something that Tom passed on to me. Jelly babies are a bit different today. They even have names now. My favourite baby is Big Heart, the blackcurrant one; then there is Boofuls, lime green, Bumper, orange, Baby Bonny, raspberry, and last but not least Brilliant, strawberry. I don't try to explain this to the kids, but I don't need to as the sweets are a hit. I hear 'jerry baby' cheerfully inserted into a conversation that I can't otherwise understand for the rest of the journey back to Bangkok. My work here is done.

In the late afternoon we reach Nong Pla Duk and connect back onto the Southern Line. When we get as far as Taling Chan Junction, I know we're almost back in the big city. I can see some of Thailand's newest trains here, the red line MRT that I'm going to try out tomorrow. The junction is modern, and wonderful if you like your buildings sterile and platforms devoid of any life – but where are the flowers, the hawkers – and, vitally, the stationmaster's bell? We leave the main line here and switch back onto the old line in the direction of Thonburi for the final leg of the journey. Looking at my map I realise that it would be perfectly possible to travel from Nam Tok to Bangkok Railway Station using Taling Chan, but Thonburi is still used for some of the best-timed trains each day. I don't know it yet, but Thonburi also holds another big rail secret.

Chapter Six
The Blues Brothers

Back in Nana the following morning I do my best to push through my morning jetlag by taking a long cold shower followed by a gloriously unhurried breakfast in my Covid-approved hotel. I'm getting used to the ritual. You arrive wearing a mask, sit down, and take it off. To venture just a few steps to the buffet requires you to put the mask back on and also don a pair of protective gloves. It's a bit of a faff, and easy to forget at this time of the day. I doubt it makes much difference to the transmission of the virus – more to reassure guests that this is a safe place. A gentleman dressed in an immaculate dark suit with a walkie-talkie earpiece has been given the delicate task of imposing these rules on the guests. I'm not a morning person, but in Asia it's my favourite time of the day. Something about the relative coolness outside, the bright sun rising and the energy of people up and about getting on with their day.

I have arranged to meet up with Richard Barrow today to spend a few hours looking around some of the newer rail projects in the city. Richard is a well-known local figure on social media, an Englishman living in Bangkok helping foreigners understand what's going on in Thailand; there can be a big void in the detail of official announcements in these parts. Our rendezvous location today is inside my local BTS station. I had offered Richard a coffee back at the hotel, but he confessed to me that he didn't want to be spotted by anyone who might recognise him on the streets of Nana, something I can now completely understand. The good news is that he likes trains, and we quickly hit it off. We form a strange double act – part Laurel and Hardy, part Dan Aykroyd and James Belushi,[10] but in a train sort of way – and spend the day whizzing all over the city on its different coloured lines. I make notes in my book and Richard posts everything we see on social media. Public transport in Bangkok is changing fast and can also be a bit confusing as the city

---

[10] from the cult 1980 film *The Blues Brothers*

gradually connects up its MRT system with its BTS system and the new rail terminus lines.

Cruising high above the pavement, we explore a few new stations in the north of the city. Up near Don Mueang Airport we switch to the brand-new dark red line; there is a light red line too. This junior school approach to colour-based naming would be much more dramatic if I ran the transport system; I would have the scarlet line, the vermilion line, even the dragon's blood line. The new electric trains on our route have open-plan carriages with huge windows for passengers to enjoy the cityscape. You would think this would be popular with commuters, but the system's not being used that much at the moment, and we have the carriage to ourselves. Besides the old airport, the line currently runs into the city only as far as Krung Thep Aphiwat Central Terminal Station, but will eventually be extended further into the centre, with plans to eventually reach Hua Lamphong. These things take time, and I admire the vision to build and connect everything up.

Today, however, our journey finishes at the Central Terminal Station. I still keep calling it Bang Sue Grand, which it technically still is, as that's what the sign says. With a swish and a whir the doors glide open, and we alight onto the futuristic platform inside the largest railway building in

South East Asia, which is also currently repurposed as a massive Covid vaccination centre. But at the moment something vital is missing – there are no other passengers. The heart of the station has not yet started beating. Today we are experimental humans to the security guards who observe us with mild suspicion from their checkpoints. One day very soon the station will open for long-distance trains, and I expect things will look very different then. Fifteen billion baht has been spent on a station building that comprises four levels, with the MRT underground, and above the ground floor a level for modern diesel trains, and on top a floor devoted to the future high-speed lines. The twenty-two platforms inside are each 600 metres long.

Richard is eager to show me some more of the city by rail, so we navigate down to the MRT. I say 'navigate', because it doesn't help that at the moment the signs in English use 'Bang Sue' to mean three different stations: the MRT station, Bang Sue Junction next door, and Bang Sue Grand. You might take signage for granted, but it can make all the difference between an easy walk and getting hopelessly lost. These signs also have to work effectively in more than one language, and things can become lost in translation. The Bangkok MRT lines form a loose reversed-Q shape around the inner part of the city. Most people are getting from A to B, but trying to do a loop of a Q is a bit tricky, and Richard and I get disoriented at the bottom of the line. Some of the route is overground, and the views give us a great perspective of parts of Bangkok that I haven't seen before.

It's been an interesting day, but I have a craving to travel further afield. First, though, I have to hang around Bangkok for yet another Covid test. This time there is no hospital visit or quarantine, and my hotel provides a PCR kit to self-test. I've thought a lot about this. If I tested positive, what would stop me from saying I'd lost the kit? ... or if I didn't even stick the swab up my nose? I don't mind doing a private self-quarantine, but I'm still fearful of the field hospital experience. I wonder how clever the system is at spotting missing PCR test results. The kit has a QR code for uploading to my online record but I think the reality of this second test is to be *seen* to be doing something without really doing very much at all. I have also met a few people who have told me they had not been able to upload their results, and no one had come to take them away in the middle of the night.

I'm over-thinking things so I decide to just do the test right now without any further contemplation. I sit down at the desk in my room and proceed. They say a watched kettle never boils, and the same is true with a PCR test. But when I return from a shower I see that a single red line has emerged. I am a now reconfirmed free man, with no more tests.

I celebrate my non-contagious status with a couple of happy hour beers in a local bar before packing my bags. I will be travelling light again on my next mission, leaving my big bag behind in Bangkok. I like the freedom of travelling light, but it's a bit weird having to remember which hotel I have left my belongings at. This thought also makes me smile. I remember my very first trip to Asia back in the 1980s when I was seriously untravelled. Back then, if you were on an organised tour from Hong Kong you could visit Guangzhou without a Chinese visa. I woke up in my Kowloon hotel bed, ate my breakfast and joined the tour group without thinking to check out. I left all my belongings unpacked in the room for four days, returning to be greeted by an irate hotel manager who almost lost his cool explaining to me the error of my ways. Nothing beats the thrill of your first trip to the Far East.

Chapter Seven
Into the Heart of Darkness

Predictably, the driver of my early evening taxi to Hua Lamphong Station wants to know where I am going. It might be just to make conversation, but also a way to suggest an alternative journey by minivan or bus, where some commission can be earned. 'Chiang Mai?' he suggests – it's by far the most popular tourist journey on board the sleeper train. 'Surat Thani?' – a stop to the south which acts as a gateway for backpackers heading for the islands. When I tell him that I'm headed for Nong Khai he gives me a knowing conspiratorial smile in the rear-view mirror. 'Visa run?' Nong Khai is a popular way of leaving Thailand for Laos and

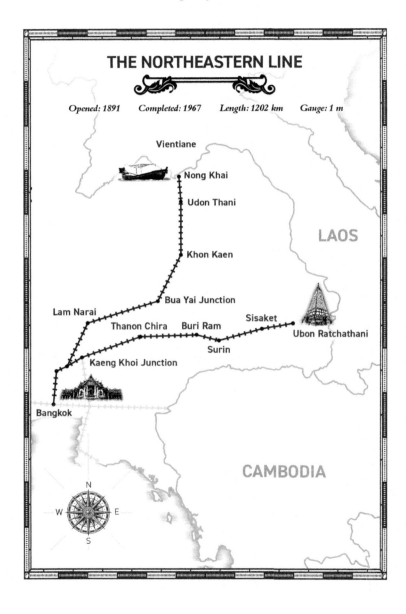

I don't feel like confusing him by explaining to him that the border is currently closed and just nod.

We stop off on the way to the station at the travel agent I'd asked to buy me a ticket in advance. I hadn't expected this train would be sold out, but I have a particular type of sleeper carriage in mind. The building is quite close to the railway station, but I don't want to have to lug my bag quite that far, so I brief the driver to wait for me and I jump out, easily finding the agent's office on the ground floor of an office block. Inside, the air conditioning whirs away behind a small mountain of plastic water bottles. I'm ushered to a seat beside the desk of a woman who has a pile of booking forms. She produces a bundle of little white tickets and marks the important bits with her pink Lumi pen. She has other colours, and I don't know if pink is a random choice or denotes something about me in her system. 'Be there one hour before,' she says, adding, 'and bring food and water.' I take a quick look over the tickets before putting them in my wallet. The ticket for tonight's train reads 'Matthew, Male, Adult, 25 Special Express CNR' and further down 'Class 1 Sleeping Coach (Air), Car 13 Seat 10 Room'. Train 25 has a single first-class carriage and tonight I will be in it. Even better, CNR signifies that it is modern Chinese-built rolling stock. I will miss the breeze blowing through an open window, but in reality, whilst open windows are good in the day they are less practical at night when the noise, weather, and light can interfere with your plans to sleep. I would have been happy in the open-plan air-conditioned second-class sleeper carriage, but tonight I've got my own room.

Feeling more relaxed and confident in my plan, I retrace my steps back to the taxi. I can't immediately see it, so I walk past a bus stop shelter to get a better view up the road. My brain then experiences one of those horrible slow-motion dawning realisations that the taxi has left without me. I'm an idiot. Adrenaline pushes me into fight mode. What are the plausible reasons for the taxi to no longer be here? Other than the dark possibility that he has just driven away with my bag, my first thought is that he has misunderstood the plan and has driven over to the railway station to meet me there. I set off with pace and urgency across the busy intersection, probably breaking any Thai jaywalking laws. With a bit of weaving and a couple of near misses I make it over to Hua Lamphong. I think I know roughly what my taxi looks like, but here at the taxi rank I realise that they all look quite similar. It's easy with hindsight, but I wish I'd written down the number. The touts sense my panic and ask me what I'm looking for, but I don't have time to explain. Realising this plan is rubbish, I abandon my search and head back

Into the Heart of Darkness

across the junction to the travel agent's office. Maybe they can call the tourist police for me? I try to take a step back from the situation and consider my options more rationally. I also try to think of warm sun and green grass to calm myself down, but it doesn't work. On the plus side, I have all my documents with me, and nothing is irreplaceable. I give myself a management pep talk to stay positive. Hopefully I'm not talking out loud, though, as I'd appear mad.

When I reach the office, I check once more the space where the taxi had been, still not quite believing how foolish I have been to get into this situation. Abandoning hope, I turn around towards the office – and there he is, waving at me on the street corner. Getting back into the taxi I breathe a sigh of relief. 'What happened?' I ask the back of his head, to which he shrugs his shoulders and kind of ignores me. Hang on … was that seat cover there before? 'Your driver had to go. I take you now,' he says. Something isn't right here. 'You have my bag?' I ask. 'Yes, we go now'. No, I'm calling it. 'Show me the bag,' I tell him, opening my door before he can pull out into the traffic. Shrugging he says 'no bag' and as I make a hasty exit he drives off.

By now my common sense is catching up with me, and I decide that calling the tourist police won't make my bag reappear any time soon. I've read somewhere that if you ever get lost in the desert you should always stay with your car rather than wandering off and perishing of dehydration trying to find help. So I decide to return to where the taxi dropped me off. There is no one here I can ask. I stand alone, looking desperately at the passing traffic.

They say that the darkest moment of the night is just before dawn, and about five minutes later a taxi pulls up in front of me. I recognise my driver, who looks pleased to see me. 'I had to drive round. Traffic police,' he tells me through the window. Thank heavens! I'm overwhelmed with relief, but also annoyed at myself for being an idiot and leaving my bag in a taxi. Actually, I'm more annoyed at myself for not remaining calm and rational when the chips were down. We drive round to Hua Lamphong and my lovely driver wishes me a good trip.

Inside the great hall of the station the atmosphere is calm and cool, in part thanks to giant fans resembling jet engines forcing cold air down from above. The low sun beams in through big glass windows and bathes the floor in a comforting evening glow. Passengers are sitting on rows of

Into the Heart of Darkness

long wooden benches waiting patiently for their trains. There is an atmosphere of the expectation of travel to faraway places by rail, the combination of camaraderie and friendliness that you never quite feel at an airport, even if you are in a comfy seat in the executive lounge. I find a spot amongst a couple of families with lots of bags behind the benches reserved for monks. In front of me I can just about see through the entrance to the platforms beneath a huge portrait of the King. To one side there is a board with the times and platforms for departing trains, mostly in Thai, but it's easy enough to work out which train is which. Hua Lamphong is going to be my home for the next couple of months, and I'm looking forward to exploring my new base, but this evening there is not enough time to do it justice.

I focus on calming down, and after a few minutes of quiet contemplation I remember a fragment of my research about the station. A couple of years ago I took a journey around the United States and wrote a book about it. It was called *Silver Streak*, a reference to a train and also a film from back in the 1970s. The big finale of the film involves a long-distance train from Los Angeles hurtling into the buffers of Chicago Union Station and crashing through a wall into the main hall. Of course, it never happened in real life, and if it did would also be technically impossible, as the hall is on a different level to the tracks. But on 11 November 1986, that actually happened – right here at Hua Lamphong. If I were sitting in this spot back then, I would have witnessed a commuter train crashing through the barriers at nearly 40 mph (64 kph) and coming to rest in the entrance hall right in front of my feet.

The train had been in for repair at the yard close to my spiritual home, Bang Sue Junction. It was one of those diesel multiple-unit trains that some countries call railcars. Six units were hitched together and the mechanic working on the third coach left the train for a break, but left the power on. Worse still, he also left the railcar in gear, and when he returned the train had gone. Once it had started moving several other mechanics had jumped off, and the train had begun a 6-mile journey towards the end of the line at Hua Lamphong, which was busy with weekend passengers. Gaining speed, it went through eight railway crossings and two stations en route to Bangkok. There was just time for the stationmaster at Bang Sue to let the stations ahead know what had happened, and urgent announcements over the platform tannoy system at Hua Lamphong managed to clear most people out of harm's way. Moments later the train hit the buffers. Three of the carriages rolled over and actually reached the main hall, taking out the departure board, the

Into the Heart of Darkness

information booth and a couple of other kiosks. Six people were reported killed in the incident. It could have been so much worse.

Then in an instant I'm back in the present day. Images of crashed carriages in my head are replaced by the bright robes of the monks sitting in front of me. I remember where I am – and, better still, where I'm going. The families around me begin to assemble their bags and keep a closer eye on the departures board, a replacement installed after 1986. The train tonight to Nong Khai is departing from Platform 3, and I decide that it's time to move, as I hate being late for anything. I'm always unfashionably early.

Passing through the entrance to the platforms I find that the train is ready to board more than half an hour before the scheduled departure time. Carriage 13 looks just like the other carriages from the outside, slightly Dan Dare fluted bare steel combined with the distinctive purple and pink stripes of the SRT sleeper carriages. A small digital display panel next to the door tells me that I'm in the right place. The outer doors are open, and I climb up and into the bright lights and air-conditioned chill of the corridor. I'm used to calling the cabins compartments in much of Europe, but like in the United States, they are called rooms in Thailand, and I find mine towards the middle of the carriage. I'm greeted by plush fuchsia fabric seats, a little folding table and a sink with a mirrored vanity cupboard above. Beside the door is a pair of screens, one for each of the two berths when they are pulled down. This will do nicely. With half an hour in hand, I drop my bag and decide to complete my pre-departure ritual of going to see the driver.

The first-class carriage is at the rear of the train, so I wander up to the front past the other second-class sleeper carriages to find the locomotive. It's quite a long way, but eventually I reach the orange and yellow Alstom 24C locomotive, which is already hooked up. The driver is in the cab doing whatever drivers do in the time before departure. Pre-departure checks, or maybe some food and social media? I wave at him, but I must appear weird, as he turns his cab lights out and ignores me in the darkness. When I return to Carriage 13 the attendant is busy distributing bedding to each of the rooms, and he says hello. The screen next to my seat now has a map of Thailand, and looks like it's going to show the live position of the train on the route. This all looks good – until I press a button with a picture of a knife and fork on it, which crashes the system and turns the screen blank. It turns out there is no official catering on this train.

Into the Heart of Darkness

I don't hear any bells ringing from inside the sleeper carriage, but we set off right on time. The ticket inspector declines my offer of a jelly baby and punches my ticket with his clippers. A few minutes later the carriage attendant offers to make up my bed and I settle down for the night. I turn the lights out and watch life passing by out the window. Bangkok beside the rails is a little eerie after dark. People sit on plastic chairs by the tracks cooking their dinner on makeshift barbecues, and televisions glare through the open doorways of the little shacks. The trackside communities on this line even have impromptu bars and little pop-up restaurants. It might not be fine dining, but it is street food with the unique outlook of passing trains. It's not long before we emerge at Bang Sue Junction, and from my side of the train the view from the window is taken up entirely by the illuminated front of the new station across the tracks.

I love the feeling of being cocooned in the comfort and privacy of a train compartment at night. When I finally pull the curtains shut and lie down, I'm left with the rhythm of the rails and the occasional flashes of light as the train passes through stations. With the door locked I'm in my own little world. Once I work out how to turn the top berth monitor off, all I can see are the illuminated buttons that control the lights and air conditioning, red dots that become distant planets in the darkness of the room. I peek through the curtains when we briefly stop at Ayutthaya, and not long after we pass by Ban Phachi Junction, taking us onto the Northeast Line. From here it's 330 miles (530 km) to the end of the rails, and time for some rest. With the regular clickety-clack of the rails sleep comes easily.

When I wake the following morning, I sense that it's early, but have to lift my airline eyeshades and squint at my phone to confirm this. Outside, wherever I am, the sun has crept above the bush and the landscape looks different to other parts of Thailand. Unfamiliar trees are dotted across the prairie like plains of scorched red earth. I could really use a cup of coffee, but there is none available on board this train. The restaurant carriages have been removed from all the express trains, and vendors boarding at stations to sell their produce don't have access to the locked and sealed first-class sleepers like as this one. The train pulls into Nong Khai 20 minutes early, at just after 6am, and I say goodbye to the attendant before climbing down onto the platform. It's like almost any other Thai station, but with one massive difference. At one end of the platform is an immigration office and a waiting area for the train onward across the Friendship Bridge to Tha Na Laeng in Laos, less than a quarter of a mile (half a kilometre) away. The

Into the Heart of Darkness

office is closed, but the commuter train is already on the other platform, and I watch a couple of people hop aboard before it trundles off towards the bridge. Although the border is officially closed, cross-border travel for locals seems to still be allowed.

Outside the station I meet a dark-skinned man wearing a wide-brimmed straw hat who shows me to his tuk tuk. It isn't the type you find in Bangkok – it's more Cambodian, the kind with a motorbike at the front towing a fixed trailer behind. I chuck my bag on and climb in, showing him a map of where I'm planning to stay. He studies the map for a while and then looks questioningly at me. He has no idea where I'm going, as my map is in English, and he can't read English, and possibly not even Thai. A small crowd gathers around to encourage him. I'm just the cargo, not a part of the debate. After a several minutes and a few shared cigarettes I can't bear it any longer, so I throw a single word into the conversation. 'Mekong,' I say loudly. There, that's a word that they all seem to understand straight away. It cuts through the vagary of a street name or a forgotten village. I feel like an explorer in search of the source of the river. But there's no doubt where the mighty Mekong is, as it meanders close by, the watery porous border between Thailand and Laos.

What I thought was quite nearby on my map turns out to be a 20-minute ride away. To make matters worse I have an emerging problem on the way to the river, as without much warning my bowels declare a digestive emergency. I hang on and hope for the best. The guesthouse looks nice, but I don't have time to admire it. In fact, I leave my bag on the tuk tuk and run for the bathroom which I intuitively guess will be down a corridor near to reception, like it nearly always is in hotels. Two doors later, and the joy of clean white porcelain. When I eventually emerge, the driver is in reception with my bag and the reception staff, I assume discussing the weakness of the Western diet. It's one of those funky outdoor reception desks that currently seems to be in fashion across the Asian hotel industry. They speak more English than I do Thai, but we have to use a phone to translate the intricacies of my booking. When Douglas Adams wrote *The Hitchhiker's Guide to the Galaxy* in 1978, the idea of a Babel Fish that you could put in your ear to understand any language in the known universe was pure science fiction, but here I am, just 40 years later, with the equivalent of the guide and the fish incorporated into my mobile phone. It turns out that the charge to check in early is more than the cost of the room for an extra night, which would have included breakfast as well. Thai hotel logic is clearly meant to ensure that no one ever checks in early, so I drop my bag and head out for a walk.

There isn't much going on in this part of town. I cross a dusty field in front of the hotel, keeping an eye out for any fierce rodents or reptiles, and climb up a concrete bank where I find a promenade along the river bank. In front of me is Laos. Small boats criss-cross the mighty Mekong delivering supplies on each side of the river. I assume that there might be a lot of tax-free trading here. In past times you might have called this smuggling. From my vantage point I can make out buildings and cars on the far bank, but not much else. Wandering along the promenade hugging the available shade, I come across a promising place to get some much-needed breakfast. I don't understand the menu, so I point to what someone else is eating, and give the lady a double thumbs-up. This gesture seems to be a safe signal for a whole bunch of positive situations and using both hands makes it much friendlier. My coffee is served in a little metal drip device called a *phin*, the kind that I have seen before in Vietnam. Coffee is really big in Thailand these days, and as long as you avoid the instant sachets of 3in1 it can taste pretty good.

I sip sweet coffee and watch the boats on the river, and a few minutes later a man on a moped pulls up outside and delivers my full Thai fry-up. The dish has been cooked in a steel frying pan, and that's what it is served in too. The fried eggs have chopped sausage on top, and on the side I have some thick slices of freshly baked French bread. What a great way to start the day.

I hitch a lift on the back of a pickup truck to take me up to the railway line near to where it approaches the bridge at the border. I just need to find the place where the lines cross the road, which turns out to be easy. There are only four shuttle trains a day, so I decide to walk along the track to see how far I can go. It's a very unassuming and rusty single track with thick bushes on each side, and there is little to see. But one day in the years ahead a new track near this point will connect Kunming in China through Laos, Thailand, Malaysia to Singapore by train.

This is big news for a landlocked country like Laos. The line from Boten on the Chinese border through to Vientiane opened in 2021, and will eventually meet a new high-speed line being constructed across Thailand, crossing the Mekong on a new bridge here at Nong Khai. The Chinese track gauge is different to most of Thailand's existing tracks, so Thailand will end up with standard-gauge high-speed lines in addition to its

Into the Heart of Darkness

existing metre-gauge network which is also being doubled up from single tracks, to speed trains up.

I love the idea of a grand South East Asian train, one that you could board in Beijing and alight from a few days later in Singapore. It should have a name, too. I'd like it to be called the Oriental Express, but a similar name is already in use by a luxury travel company, and trains with names don't seem very popular in these parts. But just like the Trans-Siberian, there will be many trains on a route with a generic name. Or more likely just a few carriages that might make the whole journey, attached to all sorts of other trains. I'm going to think of this as the Trans-Asian or the Asian Oriental Express.

The hotel finally lets me check in at lunchtime, and I take advantage of the air conditioning and crash out for a couple of hours. It's not much fun outside in the middle of the day, so I do what the locals do and stay out of the afternoon heat. When I wake up in the late afternoon I feel the need for an icy beer. Behind the market I find a Danish bar which takes its beer seriously, judging by the huge chiller cabinets on the back wall stacked with every conceivable brand of beer. I always find these nationalistic drinking enclaves interesting. Okay, you find an Irish bar and an English pub in most places – but why a Danish bar? Is it just that the owner is Danish? Or is there a reason for there to be a local Danish contingent? The answer, I discover, is both.

I choose a frosty bottle of Beerlao, a firm favourite with the Thai beer aficionados. The recipe sounds good: jasmine rice, malt from France and hops from Germany, and brewed just over the river in Vientiane. Served with a rubber jacket on the bottle, and with a frozen glass if you would like one. At these temperatures it's a standard operating procedure to put ice in your glass, but I think that's just going too far. I'll just drink my beer before it warms up. In Thailand the state owns all the big breweries and makes it hard for new brands to be established, giving Beerlao cult status. For the purposes of research I try the dark version as well as their seasonal IPA, and it's the IPA that turns out to be my favourite.

I spend the next couple of days doing very little other than sweating a lot and rehydrating with cold beer. Nong Khai is a frontier town without an international purpose right now. I'm charmed by its quiet pace of life. In the evenings I sit outside a little riverside restaurant with a cluster of street cats and watch the sunset over the banks of the Mekong. The skies here are often really dramatic just after the sun has set. I have a view of small boats travelling upriver under the Friendship

Bridge. It's right out of *Apocalypse Now*, but without any helicopters or Playboy models.

The evening train to Bangkok doesn't leave until 19.40. I'm travelling back on Special Express 26, another comfy Chinese sleeper. I'm early, so I bide my time in a layby opposite the station with half a dozen mom-and-pop places selling freshly cooked food for railway workers and passengers. Taking a seat on a chair carved out of a giant tree trunk, I ask for a beer and a menu, using international sign language. I'm having a Lawrence of Arabia moment. That scene where Peter O'Toole puts out a match between his thumb and finger, telling William Potter that the trick is not *minding* that it hurts. I'm hot, tired and sweaty, but I'm so happy to be here that I just don't care that my environment isn't particularly comfortable – this is living the life of Asian rail adventure.

At exactly 6pm the station plays the national anthem over the public address system, and everyone stops what they are doing and stands to attention. It's good over here on the tree trunk, as I can enjoy my meal but still hear the station announcements. I've barely finished my fried catfish when I hear the announcement of the shortly departing Bangkok train. Good thing I was here early. My chef puts a couple of cans of beer into a bag for me and I slip my rucksack on and wander across the road to the station. The train crew are still on parade on the platform, something that's quite routine but looks rather militaristic if you haven't seen this happen before.

I don't want to get in the way, so I stand to one side until the senior officer has taken the salute and briefed his team on tonight's train. Once this is complete I ask one of them about my train. 'Carriage 2' I pronounce carefully, holding up two fingers and my little white ticket. He points to the carriage right next to us. 'Car 2' – you get up here,' he says. But something isn't quite right. Mounting the steps, all I can see inside is an open-plan dorm-style room, constructed mostly of well-aged splintery wood. Several fans whir about on the ceiling, fighting each other to push the humid air around. Next to where I'm standing a man carefully steps down a rickety ladder from a bunk bed that looks like it has been salvaged from a WW2 prisoner of war camp. Thinking *oh dear*, I turn around and step back down onto the platform. The horror of a hot night in third class must have been written all over my face. And there was me just a few minutes ago thinking that I was made of sterner stuff. The trick is not *minding* that it's 40°C, I should be telling myself.

I find the guard again and say 'air conditioning', miming being cold by wrapping my arms around

Into the Heart of Darkness

my body. 'Car 2,' he confirms, but this time mounts the steps, gesturing me to follow him. He doesn't turn right into the dorm, but climbs down the steps on the opposite side of the carriage. On the next platform sits a gleaming set of Chinese carriages and Car 2 of the 26 Special Express. Sheepishly I thank him with a little *wai*.[11] I'm greeted by the conductor in the doorway to my carriage. 'Room 10?' he asks. I must be the only *farang*[12] in this carriage tonight.

This experience is an educational one. Firstly, it's another 'Don't panic, Captain Mainwaring' moment, and secondly, I learn that it is quite common for more than one train to depart the same place, often a fast train and a slow one, at around the same time. In this instance, Ordinary Train 134, third class, is leaving 50 minutes ahead of the Special Express, with first and second class. I also find out later that the strange carriage onboard Train 134 was actually the staff dormitory, not one for passengers.

Before we depart I watch the 134 fire-up its diesel engine, a plume of smoke rising in the purple post-sunset sky. Once it has gone a locomotive is

---

[11] traditional Thai greeting gesture, hands together and a slight bow of the head

[12] common nickname for a foreigner

shunted backwards and connected to my train. I'm calling it my train, as I'm the only passenger so far. I'm too much of a rail enthusiast to miss this operation, so even though I have changed into my dry night-time clothes I watch this from the end of platform, looking down the tracks. Some of my best train photographs come at this time of day, with fading light and the reflected colours of a towering locomotive approaching.

Back in my room I sip an illicit cold beverage and settle in. The carriage attendant makes up my bed and I share a jelly baby with him before wishing him a good night. I have seen the tiny beds that the attendants have in these Chinese carriages, and I know his night will not be as good as mine.

When I wake up, something isn't right. It's light outside and we are not moving. There is none of the soporific rattle and sway that I have become familiar with. It turns out that the train is stationary as we have already reached the stop at Bang Sue Junction. I really have slept well. Progress is, as always, slow for the last half hour, as we pass the level crossings and carve a route through the concrete jungle, pulling into Hua Lamphong right on time. This is the end of my first longer-range trip, and one that I have really enjoyed. If I can learn to handle the heat better then bigger things are possible.

Chapter Eight
The Big Mango

I moved out of Nana and into Bang Rak, a popular tourist area south of Chinatown beside the Chao Phraya River. It's fun to explore new places. Even in a single city, moving to a new district opens up new possibilities and the discovery of previously unknown places to eat, shop and hang out. But there is also a pleasure to be had in becoming a local. Someone living in the city rather than just stopping for a couple of nights. You get treated just a little bit better for your custom. I start eating at the same little food places, and become on first-name terms with the people I see each day. In the evening I usually find myself in Jack's Bar. Built on a rickety pier on the banks of the river, it provides the ideal conditions to unwind after a hot and sweaty day on the rails. There must have been some land dispute in the past, as it manages to survive squeezed between two luxury hotels. My 1928 *Guide to Bangkok* mentions one of them, The Oriental: 'The hotel is lighted all through with electric light. Special sample rooms are provided for commercial travellers. Every room in the hotel has a bath attached. The hotel maintains a steam launch at the disposal of the visitors.'

Next door at Jack's there are no baths, and the atmosphere is considerably more lively. The main attractions are cold beer, good music and an excellent spicy squid salad. It's not the sort of place that stands on ceremony, and by the end of the day most tables have small stacks of empty beer bottles to help the staff calculate the bar bills.

My usual spot is a bar table right next to the river. In bad weather this can almost be in it, as the waves splash up at your feet. I always meet interesting people here. It's a chance to exchange news of recent adventures and also to talk about trains. Everybody seems to have a rail adventure to talk about. One night I meet a gaggle of European travellers who have just come back from a place called the Mae Klong Market, also known as the Dangerous Market, the Risky Market, or the Umbrella Pull Down Market. The danger doesn't come from the umbrellas, though, but from the train which runs right through the middle of it four times each day. Getting there isn't going to be easy, but I decide that I'm going to give it a go the next day.

Noticing that I now have four empty bottles of Singha beer on my table I take this as an indication that I should probably go to bed. I point at my bottles and ask for the bill. It's an easy bit of Thai, as the words have been borrowed from English. '*Chek bin, khrap,*' I say confidently. People seem to understand even my poor pronunciation of this phrase and that it makes me feel that I can speak Thai, which of course I can't. I leave a few bank notes under an empty bottle and stand up carefully, as a large dog is lying asleep at my feet. Manoeuvring past the band and then the always happy man grilling satay, I head down the uneven stairs that lead to the dimly lit *soi*[13] outside. Out here a friendly gaggle of tuk tuk drivers offer to take me home, but the short walk helps me clear my head.

Early the next morning I get a taxi to take me to a station that I haven't been to before. It's called Wongwian Yai, named after a nearby roundabout with a large statue of King Taksin the Great. I have heard that the station is well hidden, so I have made sure the driver knows where I'm going before we set off. But it turns out that he doesn't

---

[13] side street

Bang Sue Junction

know the way, and he drops me in a busy street pointing in the general direction I need to reach the station. With no clues of where to find the place, I resort to sign language again with a couple of street vendors. This is a free comedy show for them – a farang making 'choo-choo' noises whilst pulling a pretend whistle from inside the imaginary cab of my invisible locomotive. They only get it when I start to pump my arms like a steam train with a boiler about to explode. Over a bridge, around the corner, and a few feet away I finally find the track coming up to the road at right angles. No signs or features to suggest a station, but a sudden and unexpected transition from street to rails.

Peering through a tiny hole in the wall, I speak to a lady in the ticket office, and she kindly explains what I already know. Getting a train to the market will involve not just two trains, but a boat trip across the Tha Chin River as well. This is the Mae Klong Railway, providing a line connecting the ports of Samut Sakhon and Samut Songkram to Bangkok since the early 1900s. Once part-steam and then part-electric, it is now running diesel multiple units on both parts of the line on the 40-mile run to Mae Klong at the other end.

Clutching a printed timetable and a 10-baht ticket, I sit down with a Sprite to get my head around how I'm going to do this. The problem is a

The Big Mango

Covid one. The ticket lady has crossed out some of the trains on my timetable, meaning that this journey turns out to be the least integrated transport solution that I have ever encountered. Two trains, a boat, and a half-mile walk between them, and a timetable that means spending hours sitting about making connections. Worst of all, if I want to see the train arrive at the market from the ground, I will have a three-hour wait for a returning train. Slightly depressed by this discovery, I decide to wave the white flag on this one for now. I need a Plan B.

Bright and early the following morning, I try again, but this time with a new solution, a minivan and a lady called Kiwi, who has offered to take me to meet her mother who has a trackside stall in the market. She introduces me to our driver, who is called Apple. It's not a family fruit fetish, but Thai recognition that foreigners find Thai names very hard to remember, let alone pronounce, so many Thais adopt an easy Western name as well; it makes me consider whether I should have a Thai nickname to balance up this cultural kindness. Today is clearly going to be a fruit-themed day, as her mother is called Mango. Not only that, but Kiwi also explains that like New York being called the Big Apple, Bangkok is known to many as the Big Mango.

Bang Sue Junction

I'm sad not to be on a train, but this plan saves hours of hanging about. I'll come by train another time. We make good progress on the busy Bang Na Expressway, and reach Mae Klong in time for the arrival of the late morning train. The station here is just like Wongwian Yai – one minute you're on a busy street, then around the corner you're in a railway station now squashed on all sides by urban sprawl. The station has notices hung up on every spare space on its walls. The place oozes practicality rather than prettiness. In the middle of the platform hangs a big bell; it's not the shiniest I have seen, and has clearly seen a lot of action. Close behind an almost life-size portrait of the King stands on top of a stage festooned with much golden tinsel. Above the entrance to the little waiting room behind, the largest sign of all proclaims 'Beware of taking photos while the train is passing'. I have seen a few signs at Hua Lamphong that prohibit photography altogether, so this is a new one on me. The next time I see Richard Barrow I ask him about this, and get the impression that it applies to commercial photographers, as wedding parties occasionally descend on the station to have their pictures taken. This is not something you would see at Liverpool Street or Kings Cross.

The market is on the other side of the station, so trains pass through it to reach the platform.

The Big Mango

Switching them around would undoubtedly save a lot of time and perhaps a few lives, but that's just not how things work here. Kiwi gives me a health and safety pep talk, after which we hop down onto the track and walk up the line. Stooping under a dense canopy of overlapping umbrellas, we find ourselves, once our eyes have adjusted, in a packed wet market with writhing seafood in polystyrene containers and buckets on both sides of the single line. It's the kind of setup you find all over Asia, just that this one has got a railway running through the middle of it. The only way through the market is on the track, but even here it's hard to make progress whilst avoiding the carts being wheeled along the rails in both directions. The people running the stalls must be fed up with people like me who have no real plans to buy a bag of crabs here today.

About halfway along the market track we step into a small stall and Kiwi introduces me to Mango, who is going to look after me when the train arrives. At first I felt this is a bit over-protective, but a full safety briefing follows that helps me understand why. I must at all costs stand the width of three of the concrete slabs away from the track. Kiwi makes me practise this like a kid's counting game. 'One, no – two, no – three, safe,' she makes me repeat several times and then do a hopscotch before she is convinced I'm not going to become a tourism accident statistic. Mango directs me to a low plastic stool to sit on and offers me a slice of watermelon, which is a welcome treat here amidst the oppressive atmosphere of crowds of people with nowhere to stand and the overwhelming stench of fish guts.

You hear the train's horn before you see it as the driver has to slow right down for the transformation that is about to take place. In a display of synchronised umbrella removal, the shades and tarps above us are pulled back, revealing the sky. Our subterranean world is now exposed to the heat of the sun; while the trays of fruit and vegetables right up to the track are left where they are, the bigger boxes of fish are pulled back inside the shop houses. I find a slab of concrete to stand on, which I calculate is far enough back. Mango approves of my position and I wait to see what happens next. Small groups of tourists around me search in vain for a space to get off the line as the engine rumbles slowly towards us. I don't get to see their fate, as before I know it my nose is just a couple of inches away from the side of the locomotive. Looking down at my feet, I realise that the bodies of the carriages are far wider than the track and are passing right over our garlic and chilli crops. My sunburned toes are just a few inches behind them. As soon as the last carriage passes, selfie-crazed tourists pop out from behind to film the shades going back up again. Two minutes later, if it were not for the track you would never know that a train had just passed through. The fusing together of everyday life with edgy tourism has created a near-perfect health and safety storm here. Influencers put pressure on each other for the perfect and probably most dangerous-looking photograph in front of the oncoming train for a few more clicks on social media.

Back at Jack's Bar I share my experiences with this evening's crowd. A man who introduces himself as Joseph tells me that there is a similar place in Hanoi, where the restaurants are right alongside the tracks. It was shut down recently after another near miss. The official reason given was that it wasn't meeting its 'fatality quota'. Rubbing salt into the wounds of health and safety, a policeman on the barrier of the closed road was quite badly hurt as he was playing Candy Crush on his phone when a train approached at speed. But the pressure of tourism has since allowed train street to reopen. We live in a mad world.

Back in my hotel room I pack my bags ready for one of my shorter missions – a trip to explore the part of the Eastern Line that heads south to the tourist mecca of Pattaya. If only I'd known what was to come.

Bang Sue Junction

Chapter Nine
Combat Rock

The Eastern Line has been constructed in several phases, the first branch opening in 1907. Its 158 miles (254 km) of track connect Bangkok to the Cambodian border and to the Northeastern Line at Kaeng Khoi Junction, and also down to the Gulf of Thailand, to the port at Map Ta Phut, a vital freight connection. I'm headed to Pattaya today, but to the international rail traveller it is the Cambodian branch that is probably the most interesting. The line first reached Aranyaprathet, close to the border, in 1926. In 1941 it actually extended onwards into Cambodia for a few miles. This was closed at the end of the Second World War, opened again in 1955, then closed again as a result of worsening political relations. A new link

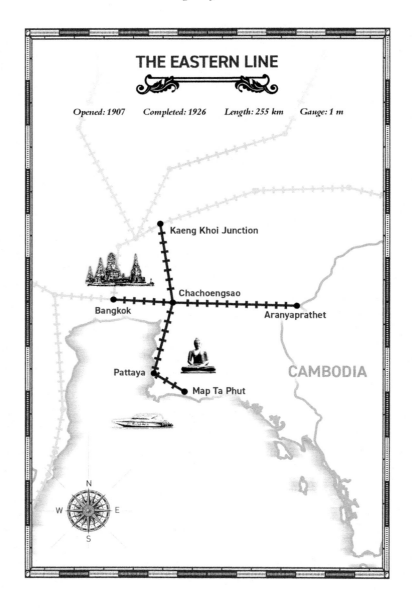

Combat Rock

taking the Thai line back up to the border at Poipet was opened in 2019, but at the time of writing is closed as a result of the pandemic.

A few years ago I travelled from Edinburgh to Singapore by land and sea, pretty much all the way by train. It was an epic journey, and I ended up writing a book about it: *A Bridge Even Further*. Things have changed quite a bit since that trip. As well as the border connection there is also now a rail link between Poipet and Phnom Penh. But back then I had to travel across Cambodia by bus then taxi to reach the border town of Poipet, breaking the otherwise continuous rails from IJmuiden, my landfall on Eurasia, to Singapore.

If you ever saw the first film in the original Star Wars trilogy, you might remember Obi-Wan Kenobi's warning to Luke Skywalker about Mos Eisley Spaceport: 'You will never find a more wretched hive of scum and villainy. We must be cautious.' Poipet is a very similar place, and you don't want to hang about in it for very long. The clues are there long before you arrive at the frontier. Billboards line the road not for advertising duty free shopping but warning of the penalties for animal and drug smuggling. There are no bounty hunters here, but plenty of touts selling expensive visas and transportation packages to faraway places. Other than crossing the border, the only

Bang Sue Junction

other reason to visit Poipet would be to gamble in one of the 24-hour casinos on the Cambodian side of the frontier town. I'm no gambler, but I checked one out and it was pretty depressing. Inside the darkened interior there was no sense of time, as the management want you to stay there until you run out of money. The mostly Thai businessmen wandered around like zombies. I didn't see anyone who looked even faintly happy.

Once in Thailand the journey by train to and from Bangkok is relaxed and friendly enough. There are just two Ordinary third-class trains a day, and for less than 50 baht you get a four-hour journey through the countryside with an open window. Some joke and call this train the Cambodian Express, which it isn't, as it's very slow and doesn't even make it as far as the border. In the next couple of years it is likely that there will be a direct train service between Bangkok and Phenom Penh on this route, and if it comes to be I hope it will be called the Real Cambodian Express.

Most Bangkok minivan drivers would like to have you believe that the Eastern Line branch doesn't even exist, but from Bangkok it actually only takes 2½ hours on it to reach the beach at Pattaya. Inside Hua Lamphong it takes just a couple of minutes to get a ticket for the 997 Rapid service, which costs 170 baht. That seems a bit pricey in the pre-coffee fog of my brain, but it is for a seat in an air-conditioned second-class carriage, and on a train that is faster than the normal timetable. Technically this is known as a Rapid, a train for transferring city dwellers to the beach at weekends. As I head out onto the platform, the train that is standing at Platform 6 looks rather familiar. On a need-to-know basis it's a Class 158, the sort that might take you to Portsmouth Harbour or Peterborough back home. Thailand bought twenty of these carriages from British Rail in 1990 and converted them to run in a rather different setting.

Despite being early morning once again, it's already busy on board. I find my reserved seat in Carriage C by the sealed window. Rather than the metal shutters in third class, here I have curtains that have seen better days, and a little table that folds down from the back of the seat in front. The air conditioning is on the Arctic setting, and I wish I had packed a jumper. It's a bank holiday weekend, and families escaping Bangkok fill the carriage with strollers, inflatables and all kinds of stuff, mainly in colourful plastic bags. There is an air of excitement and anticipation of the weekend ahead, and it is nice to be part of this. Parents chat and take selfies, kids hunker down in their seats and stream shows on their phones. I'm on my own

Bang Sue Junction

in looking out the window and making notes in my book.

I can't hear any bells this morning, but at 06.45 the driver revs the engine dramatically and engages the drive. It sounds like an underpowered truck with a dodgy clutch, and he has to give it full beans to get us away from a standing start. We don't reach the advertised sprinter speed for the first few miles as the train is having to tackle the busy Bangkok road crossings. But this suits me, as I'm looking out for a few landmarks along the way. Our first stop is at Makkasan Station. This is the home to one of the main workshops for the SRT, and on the other side of a wall I can see the carcasses of old trains, a graveyard of rusting diesel locomotives. I'd like to see more of this place.

Back in 1982 on a Sunday evening I would busy myself recording the charts from the radio onto a cassette tape whilst eating lots of hot buttered toast. The trick was to try and edit out the talk bits of the chart show by pre-emptively guessing when to press the stop button. You also had to contend with occasional incidents of either tangled tape or hot butter in your cassette mechanism. I'm too embarrassed to tell you the sort of things that I listened to back then, but it definitely wasn't The Clash, and I had no awareness of their fifth studio album and its railway significance.

122

Just past Makkasan, underneath the modern concrete spans of the airport rail link, is the location I'm looking for. It's pretty much impossible to judge accurately from inside the carriage, but spiritually this feels right. I'm getting that sense of place again: it's the spot where Pennie Smith took the now iconic shot that was used on the cover of The Clash's *Combat Rock* album. The band stayed at the Bangkok Palace Hotel behind the station for nearly two weeks on their 1982 world tour, recovering from various tropical diseases and addictions. I checked the place out, and without being too critical I would say that it's no longer a venue that rock bands would choose to stay in today. Strange how some hotels live on as the place to stay, whilst others fade away to mediocrity.

I have a CD copy of the album with me in my bag, which I get out to try to identify the very spot where the picture was taken. The kids opposite me have probably never seen a CD before, so I let them have a look. No one else in the carriage has their camera out to photograph this special location. Sadly also, no one seems interested in having a debate about the legacy of The Clash.

This train is fast but rather soulless – neither ultra-modern and comfortable like the new Chinese rolling stock, nor old school and characterful like the ordinary third-class carriages. The upside is that it is an hour and a half faster than the standard train. It makes me feel like a commuter rather than traveller, someone in too much of a hurry to get to their destination. But when we eventually pull into Pattaya my mood lifts somewhat as the sun is shining and I'm looking forward to a spot of late breakfast.

I realise my mistake as soon as a minivan drops me off at the front of the glitzy-looking beachfront hotel, where I am faced with a procession of cars disgorging family groups, and a bellboy overwhelmed with the belongings that you need for a weekend break by the seaside. I make the taxi driver let me get out without waiting to reach the front of the queue of cars at the hotel's entrance. Inside are a squad of full-size furry animal characters waiting to greet me, which I manage to avoid by reaching reception from around the side of the foyer. The lady behind the desk looks at me across the desk with a mixture of concern and sympathy when she sees I'm on my own. I'm a massive round peg in a very square hole here. I have misunderstood the meaning of a Thai family-friendly hotel. The reason I booked this place was to be insulated from the sleaze of the city, but I'm as far out of my comfort zone here as in the underbelly of Pattaya's infamous nightlife.

The beach outside is hidden from view by a solid block of beach umbrellas to keep the Thai tourists fully covered from the sun. Underneath the umbrellas is a tight maze of tables and chairs in the sand, and in here I find someone who takes my order for breakfast. I can't stay here for long, though. It's suffocating, and the sand sticks to my sweaty legs, attracting the flies.

Over the road I pass a sunburned European man wearing a football vest and a lot of gold jewellery. He introduces himself as Stanley and asks me where I'm going. Normally I'd take this to be the sure beginning of a scam, but he appears to me as an authentic expat living the life of his dreams. I tell him I'm looking for a shady place to relax and take the opportunity to find out where to eat and drink in this part of the city. He tells me he only knows about go-go bars and women, and he's astonished to learn that I have plans for neither during my stay. 'Why else would you come to Pattaya?' he asks me. It's a fair question.

I stroll down the road until I spot the familiar sight of a foot massage parlour. There are not many takers for a foot massage at this time of the day, and I'm soon lying back in a big leatherette reclining chair having my feet washed and scrubbed. Some people don't like having their feet touched, but I find it one of the biggest bargains of life in Thailand. An hour of possibly health-giving massage and a cup of tea for less than 200 baht. You can't go wrong. I often take a nap, but today I join the others in watching an episode of the latest Thai soap opera on the television screen above the shrine. All massage places have shrines; this one isn't as elaborate as some I have seen, but it does have a small pond complete with the effect of a cloud of smoke on the surface. The soap opera is hard to follow, but it looks like there is a problem at work and the leading male character is bringing the trouble he's in back to his family at home, who sit around the kitchen table discussing things for most of the show. This is interspersed with ad breaks for supermarket offers, then the show runs a recap in case we are goldfish and have forgotten the story so far. I let the staff know that I'm having problems trying to follow the plot, and they find this funny as they can't understand it either.

When I return to the hotel I finally get a key to my room – but only once I have agreed with them what time I will have breakfast tomorrow. Apparently, the restaurant has several sittings to avoid excess crowds. My room is modern and mainly painted white. White walls, white furniture, white floor. I put my sunglasses on. Pulling back the white curtains I'm greeted by a scene of true horror. A brigade of children are having a water fight on a pirate island right in front of my room.

Combat Rock

Their water cannon doesn't quite reach my window, which is a saving grace of the setup. It turns out that I'm staying at a water theme park. My chances of a relaxing few lengths of the pool and a lie-down are going to be nothing more than a fantasy here. Nearby, a queue of kids wait their turn to drop down a water slide, but only when the lifeguard signals they can go by blowing his whistle – every 30 seconds. I draw the curtains closed and take a seat at my white desk in a white chair and think what to do. I wish I was back in Bangkok.

Thai people strike me as a tolerant and non-judgemental race, and Pattaya has to be the ultimate testing point of this. It's early in the post-pandemic recovery of Thailand, but the girlie bars down on Walking Street are already back doing a roaring trade. Pattaya is adult tourism on an industrial scale. All I'm seeking is a place to have quiet beer and read my trusty copy of *On Track* by Paul Grittens, an account of Henry Grittens, a Siam Railway construction pioneer. I'm not even near the main part of the red light district but yet I'm getting grabbed and pulled into places that I have no interest in frequenting. I go as far as to have a beer at a table outside one of the more harmless looking bars, and within minutes I'm fighting off half a dozen overly amorous bar girls. I'm a veteran of Nana, but the combination of family hotels and concentration of adult tourism here seems like a very strange mix. A Thai version of Blackpool and old Soho coexisting, but on steroids.

The following morning the man by the pool with the whistle wakes me earlier than I would have liked. I had figured that an early breakfast might be more peaceful on a Sunday morning, but I'm wrong; when the lift door opens at the restaurant level I'm greeted by a sea of hungry people waiting to be seated. Most are wearing plastic gloves and face masks, but they have no way of avoiding close contact with fellow diners. I don't have a booking for this sitting, but hope that the staff won't challenge me if I just stroll in, and I'm right. I fight my way up to the hotplate without bumping into anyone, or more accurately them bumping into me. There is little spatial awareness here. Whirling Dervishes carrying plates piled high with scrambled eggs spin past as I aim for the toaster. Like many hotel toasters it has a sign on it telling people not to push croissants into it, but the woman in front of me jams several in, and when only one of them pops out underneath help is required to put the fire out. Then I put a couple of slices of white bread in, which return as slices of white bread, a process I repeat three times before they have any sign of becoming toast.

My mission today is an escape plan. I'm going to head back to Bangkok on the 998 Rapid. That gives me a few hours to kill, which I mostly spend writing notes and reading up on my next destination, Chiang Mai, somewhere which I hope will be a complete antidote to Pattaya. I manage a swim in the hotel pool, the trick being to time my length so that the full-sized flying bomb children don't land directly on top of me at the end of their pipe ride. When I arrive at the checkout desk the manager on duty asks me if I enjoyed my stay. I shrug my shoulders and diplomatically explain the reason for my shortened stay. It's not the hotel's fault, I just misunderstood what 'family-friendly' means. Lesson learned, I'll always look at photos of the pool before booking a resort hotel like this in the future.

I need transport to get back to the railway station, but the hotel wants to charge an eye-watering fee for the privilege of fixing a taxi for me. The first one I find out on the street is a car parked up with the driver asleep. I tap on the window and ask him how much to the railway station. A bleary-eyed response: '400 baht'. I counter-offer the price twice: 'Okay, 200, but not the bus station.' 'You know where it is?' he asks me. 'No,' and with that I move on. I try several more, but none of them know where the train station is, or even, in fact, that Pattaya is connected to Bangkok by a railway

Bang Sue Junction

line. But eventually I find a woman with a pickup truck who knows about the station. It turns out that it isn't an obvious place to reach going out of the city, as the planners have assumed everyone will arrive in town on the shiny new expressway. However, she takes a few turnings down back alleys and we arrive at the station with ease.

Now that I have more time to look around than on my arrival, I see that this really is a model of everything that is good about Thai railway stations. Spotlessly clean, plenty of wooden benches on the single long platform, well-kept flower beds, and a stall selling cold drinks. Once again at the centre of the operations is the super-helpful stationmaster and his shiny bell. If there were a competition for shiny bells this one would be in the semi-finals. A few minutes after I have sat down in the shade he announces a train in Thai, but it's too early to be the Number 997. It's a freight train carrying oil from the nearby port to the rail yard on the outskirts of Bangkok, and he green flags it straight through. The next train sounds more promising: '4.30 to Hua Lamphong?' I ask him, pointing at my watch. 'No,' he says with a shake of his head, 'next train is the 4.26 to Bangkok, this platform.' It's a very Swiss response, if you believe that Swiss trains are as punctual as folklore suggests.

We set off on time, bouncing on the springs of the multiple unit as we build up speed. Topping 60 mph, we flash through rural stations, stopping only at a few bigger towns along the way. The sun begins to set and the fields are bathed in the late afternoon light. But as we approach Bangkok the sky begins to turn black and it's not long before I experience my first flood in the city. In the English language there are many ways to describe rain, and I think there is just one for this type: biblical. The roads running parallel to the tracks quickly become rivers, but the locals press on riding their mopeds through the water as though they have been supplied with specially converted amphibious models. Our train splashes across the level crossings but then has to wait for an hour or so at a station halt. There is a special flood procedure which involves people dressed in flimsy yellow raincoats and flip-flops brushing the water away with big straw brooms. When enough sweeping is deemed to have taken place, the bell rings, the train revs up again and we proceed very slowly on the final stretch of the waterlogged tracks into a comfortingly dry platform at Hua Lamphong. I'm back in Jack's Bar for dinner, and it's time to exchange experiences of my weird weekend.

Bang Sue Junction

Chapter Ten
Elephant Man

It's not long before I'm back at Hua Lamphong for the next night train, this time to Chiang Mai. The more I use Bangkok Station, the more I realise how much that I'm going to miss it when it's no longer the departure point for long-distance trains. The temperature-check man at the entrance waves me inside like an old friend. This is quite special, as I have a theory that just as Westerners think Asian people all look very similar, so it must be true the other way around.

I have already bought my ticket from the agent across the street, as this is the most popular sleeper train in Thailand and I didn't want to leave anything to chance. It's been printed in Thai, but the lady in the office has written the important stuff

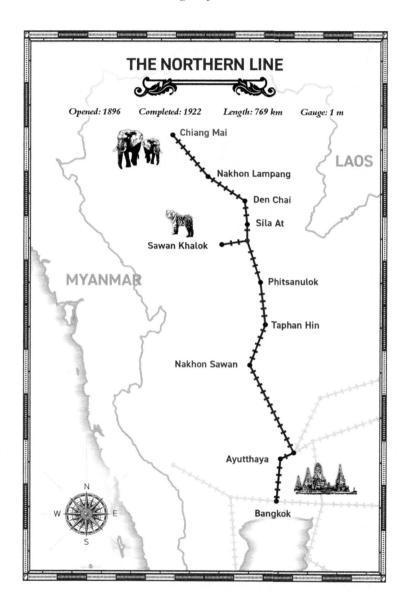

on the ticket in English. This is Special Express Number 9. There are several trains going to the end of the Northern Line each day, but this one, like the train I took to Nong Khai, uses the newer Chinese carriages. The timings are perfect, leaving Bangkok at just after 6pm and arriving the following morning at around 7am. Costing 2453 baht (£55), my first-class sole-occupancy room isn't exactly cheap, but if you think about it as a night in hotel, it's actually a bit of a bargain. In many ways this is the perfect route for a sleeper train, ideal for an early evening departure and a breakfast-time arrival if all has gone to plan overnight. It's also very viable because Chiang Mai is such a big tourist pull, and the train provides an eco-friendly and fun means of transport that the plane just cannot match. I find my usual place on a bench in the waiting area of the hall behind the monks once again. There is no need to rush: no ticket checks before getting on the train, no barriers, no secrecy until the last moment about the platform number. Those are backward Western ways.

I have a new bit of kit with me this evening, but before I tell you about it I'd like to briefly mention the history of the wonderful Thai railway dining car. Thai restaurant carriages used to be the social centre of long-distance trains and an immensely rewarding part of any long journey. My 1928 *Guide to Bangkok* says 'The Royal State Railways of Siam take great pride in their restaurant car service and experienced cooks are employed to serve a wholesome and excellent cuisine'. I have fond memories, from my 2014 trip to Singapore, of a full waiter service offering everything from an icy Chang beer at sunset through to a freshly cooked breakfast at my seat from an extensive menu complete with a picture of each dish. It didn't get much better than at-seat dining with an amazing and ever-changing view. Later on in the evening, there was a karaoke party in the dining carriage itself. Those were the days. Very sadly, one night in July that year everything changed when a girl on the sleeper headed down to Surat Thani was murdered by a drunk railway employee. That single incident led to the banning of alcohol on all trains and railways stations in Thailand. One knock-on effect of this was that the dining cars were not nearly as profitable without alcohol sales, and as franchises, no one wanted to run one any more. Then the pandemic delivered the final blow. I'm sure they will be back soon. The rumour is that they will be reborn as simpler and more modern cafes. In the meantime, vendors board the open carriages constantly, sell their wares, then hop off at the next stop. But in the sealed air-conditioned sleeper carriages necessity has been the mother of invention, and now the guard will take an order for a meal that will be delivered at a platform down the line. It's similar to the system that works so well in India, albeit with less choice.

After my experience of no catering on the Nong Khai sleeper, I have made my own plan. It came from my very first experiences on the Trans-Siberian a few years ago, when I staggered into Moscow's Yaroslavsky Station with almost a week's provisions, which it turned out I would barely need. But I like to be prepared. So, earlier today I visited a local Bangkok department store and bought a coolbox, the plastic kind with a handle that you take on a family picnic. Mine is now filled with ice from 7/11 and a good selection of cold beverages.

I'm going to be staying in Chiang Mai for a few weeks, so this time I have all my belongings with me. The small mountain of baggage piled up next to me needs to be loaded onto the train, so I give up my seat and shuffle forwards in the direction of the platform. This turns out to be a schoolboy error, as firstly the train isn't at the platform yet, secondly there is no air conditioning out here, and thirdly there is no seating, either. I'm not alone hoping that the train will appear soon, as the platform is already busy with backpackers. Big rucksacks, singlets, yoga pants, flip-flops and strange hair, the whole smash. I suspect that

I might be the only person here without a piercing or at the very least a tattoo. I envy them, as I didn't leave Europe when I was a student – the closest I got to Asia was a couple of days in Istanbul. These days the rites of passage for gap year trips and even holidays are far grander.

The sleeper train team is a well-oiled machine this evening. Staff pull up cages of freshly laundered bedding and supplies to the exact positions on the platform where the sleeper carriages will stop, ready for work like a motor racing pit stop. All we need is the train. Which is, unusually for a Bangkok departure, late. I pass the time chatting with a few fellow passengers to find out what their plans are. Jungle trekking, mountain biking, elephant conservation, all the things that the north of Thailand has to offer. My coolbox gets a few admiring glances, and one American lady says she has never seen someone with so much luggage. I take that as a compliment, but it probably wasn't meant to be one. We wait together at a place where there is a barely perceptible movement of air; the ventilation system in the hall is touching this spot but no other place on the platform. It remains our secret from the sweaty backpackers all around us. I look out for the train down the line, as though looking for it will make it arrive sooner. It's hard-wired into my brain to look for things like this, attempting to fix the

Elephant Man

uncertainty of what's going to happen next. Then I spot a train around the slight bend in the tracks outside the station, and as it gets closer it looks like it's heading for our platform. It's being pushed back in at a walking pace. Everyone can see it when it reaches the shade of the station roof, and people are jostling to reach the position of their carriage on the platform. As soon as the train comes to a stop at the platform the crew immediately get to work, swarming around the open doorways. Their pace and urgency transmit a false sense of needing to rush to get on board, so I hang back whilst the supplies are loaded. There is good reason for this. I'm going to need space to help to get my bags on. The station has low platforms, and the floor height of the carriage is above my shoulders. The two steps up are fine without big bags, but it's a whole new logistical exercise with heavy lifting. But I need not have worried; the guards spot my need and gesture me to climb up, swinging my bags up behind me with biomechanical expertise and evidence of regular gym attendance.

The atmosphere on board is friendly, and I'm sure that the crew on this route are very used to looking after the needs of foreign tourists. My decadent request for an extra pillow is no problem, and I decide to get my bed made up early so I can relax in peace and quiet. By the time we leave the station we are running half an hour late and it's dark outside, but I still manage to spot the trackside landmarks that I'm learning to recognise. Darkness briefly turns back to light when we arrive at Bang Sue Junction. Not from Bang Sue itself, but from the towering illuminations of Krung Thep Aphiwat Central Terminal next door. At night it definitely looks even more like an alien spacecraft. It also reminds me of Berlin Hauptbahnhof, where at night time glittering trains arrive up in the air on invisible elevated lines and enter the building entrance holes as if they were spacecraft.

As we pull out of the station I poke my head out of the door to my room. All seems quiet up and down the carriage now. I have obviously missed the moment when it became socially acceptable to play music and sports games out loud on mobile devices in public places, and South East Asia is at the centre of this failure in sonic etiquette. On sleeper trains this can be even more tricky, as passengers think they are in a soundproofed room, which is actually a total illusion. The French couple next door have been streaming a cartoon film on maximum volume, but they seem to have gone to bed now. When I take a stroll down to the toilets at the end of the corridor all the compartment doors are closed and even the attendant has turned in for the night.

When I talk to people about how much fun long-range rail trips are, the conversation often turns to concerns about 'the facilities'. Perhaps this is a throwback to the Victorian obsession with the water closet devised by Thomas Crapper. In the past I have been faced with some pretty grim toilets in Siberia and distant Chinese provinces, but on board this modern carriage tonight, I have the choice of well-maintained toilets and separate shower rooms. There is even a little indicator on the screen in your room that tells you when each of them is free. You probably don't want to know too much about the way train toilets function, but it's worth mentioning that whereas older trains just dump waste straight onto the tracks, modern carriages have pressurised systems with an aircraft-style flushing system and holding tanks. These reduce environmental impact and better protect rail workers, but have a habit of breaking down owing to passenger misuse. Modern stations like Krung Thep Aphiwat Central Terminal will only service trains with these new systems. This is important, as it means that older-style carriages on local trains arriving in Bangkok will have to use Hua Lamphong for some time to come.

Back in my room, I double-lock the door and open up my minibar. I have a bit of a guilty feeling about transgressing the no-alcohol rule, but who's going to notice? Holding an icy can of my favourite beverage in my hand, I attempt to open the ring pull at a moment disguised by another noise, but totally fail. In the now quiet carriage I fear that everyone knows that someone has just opened a can of something cold and frothy. But there are no knocks at the door, and I spend an hour or two watching the stations flash past in the night. At Ban Phachi Junction we part from the Northeastern Line and turn northwards towards Chiang Mai, which is as far north as the tracks go in Thailand. Content with everything, I pull the curtains and slide down in my bed, quickly drifting off into the usual mix of railway dreams and nightmares, mostly about being on a rollercoaster interspersed with losing my bag or missing my train.

I rise at daybreak so that I can witness the scenery of the jungle of Northern Thailand. The only significant problem with taking the sleeper train to Chiang Mai is that you miss a lot of the amazing scenery in the night. But just after 6am everything turns black again. Not an eclipse, but the sign that we have entered the Khun Tan Tunnel, the longest in Thailand, at 1362 metres. This had been a grim job for the Chinese and Lao coolies to build in the snake- and leech-infested jungle of what is now a national park. More than 1000 workers are said to have died of cholera and malaria during the eleven years of its construction before it opened in 1922. From the tunnel it is a further 42 miles (68 km) onward to Chiang Mai, and at just after 07.30 we pull into the station, now just a few minutes behind schedule. My final job before packing and getting off the train is to dispose of the couple of kilos of ice weighing my coolbox down. I tip it into the little sink in my room, hoping the evidence will melt before anyone questions what I might have been up to.

It feels unusually cool on the platform, certainly a different climate to Bangkok. I offer a goodbye jelly baby to the carriage attendants and drag my bags from the far end of the platform into the station building. Chiang Mai Station actually has a turntable dating back from the age of steam, but these days it is unused as the diesel locomotives are uncoupled and reversed along a siding to join the other end of the carriages, ready to return in the opposite direction. The place today has an eclectic mix of exhibits from the past, modern cartoon characters and some colourful gardening. There is of course also a big shiny bell just in front of the buffers. There should be a name for this eclectic station design style. I'm going to call it Thai Railway History & Theme Park Fusion.

A scrum of songthaew drivers are ready and waiting to ambush passengers outside the station entrance. They are hungry for as many tourists looking for a lift into town as they can squeeze in. Ignoring their advances I walk past the negotiations, as right in the middle of the car park is Locomotive Number 340, manufactured in Switzerland in 1912. Then almost before I've even said the words 'can I get a ride into town?', I'm in the back of a van with a couple of Japanese girls who seem more afraid of me than the snappy dog in the cab. I'm pleased that I've had a recent course of rabies jabs.

I wander around the deserted streets of the old walled city for the rest of the morning. In these parts tourism is a major part of the economy, and it has not bounced back yet. To pass the time I take part in a couple of activities, one pleasant and one not. I treat myself to a full 'British Isles' breakfast at a British pub. Try not to judge me; sometimes you just need a taste of home. Then I find a massage parlour just along the street. My shoulder has been giving me some pain lately and I need to get it fixed. The mama-san at the desk listens to my description of what's wrong. Her diagnosis is the nuclear one. A full head, neck and shoulders routine at maximum Thai strength. None of that nice relaxing Swedish stuff. The treatment will take an hour, and by the end she says it will hurt for the next day or so, then I will be cured. It's an hour of almost unbearable pain, but I'm determined not to have to ask for it a bit softer. At one point when the tiny lady masseuse digs her elbow under my shoulder blade I almost start to cry, but the endorphins must have kicked in as I make it to the end without giving in. I'm going to have to learn the Thai word for 'softer'.

Keen to try my hand at learning to make railway rice, I sign up for cookery school in the afternoon. In their office a couple of ladies present me with a bingo calling card of different courses, each with its own set of daily dishes. I'm spellbound by the choices and their enthusiasm, so I sign up for a whole week as I like the look of all of them. Learning to cook Thai could be a new religion.

Railway fried rice is an institution in Thailand. It emerged into Thai culinary culture as the railways of the kingdom expanded and people needed something simple and tasty to eat on the move. Japan might have its bento box and Britain its buffet cheese sandwich, but here in the kingdom of smiles, it's fried rice. The recipe is really simple. Fry off some precooked jasmine rice and add sliced onion, eggs, fish sauce, dark soy sauce, garlic, sugar and coriander. Then serve with some chilli, fish sauce, cucumber, tomato and a small wedge of lime on the side. If you're lucky you might get a fried egg served on top. The rich flavours combined with a chilli kick are amazing.

The office next door to the cookery school is the kind of place that you find all over South East Asia. It sells all sorts of tourist trips on commission, but don't hold that against them. A man called Israel – who happens to be from Israel – hands me a plastic file, and points to a few tours he thinks I might like. All the usual activities are represented, and most of them are quite jungly. Zip lining, shooting, rafting, trekking and biking, as well as the ubiquitous minivan temple tours. One thing I can't see here are elephant rides, and I ask Israel why. He explains that in recent years there has been a shift to more responsible tourism. The problem was that the tourism trade had turned elephants from productive agricultural workers into living tuk tuks exploited for lucrative profits. When that practice was called out for what it was, the negative publicity drove a much-needed shift towards conservation. Now it's no longer acceptable to go on an elephant ride, but great to camp alongside working elephants and to wash them down in the warm muddy rivers each day.

I have never been on a serious zip line, so choose one that allows you to fly high over the jungle canopy. When I tell Israel my choice, he goes out to the back of the shop and returns with a set of weighing scales, encouraging me to hop on. It turns out I'd need to go on a diet for a couple of weeks to make the weight, something that isn't going to be compatible with my cookery course. My second choice is mountain biking, which gets his approval, and he books me on to a local ride for the following morning.

There is a good expat network here in Chiang Mai, and it's easy to make new friends. You can quickly become a local in a bar of your choosing, with the perks of a reserved seat and complimentary peanuts. My local is a bar in the night market, and that evening I tell a couple of new friends of my plans. When I show them the colourful brochures, one guy points out that a man recently died on the zip line ride as the cable failed. The bike ride also has a high casualty rate. It turns out I have signed up to bike down Doi Suthep, a mountain as high as Ben Nevis. I try to put this to the back of my mind and consume freshly fried cashew nuts with my beer to the sounds of well curated 70s rock music.

It's cold the next morning — really cold for the locals, who are all wearing sweaters and knitted hats. To me it's just cool, and a welcome respite from the oppressive heat of Bangkok. Nursing a seriously stiff shoulder from yesterday's massage, I wait in the reception of my hotel for the mountain bike people. Before too long a man arrives with a big pickup truck and I scramble up into the back. The van fills up as we collect more tourists from their hotels and guesthouses around the city. What is alarming is that most of them are dressed in lycra. It takes about an hour to reach the top of the mountain by winding road, and it's even colder at this altitude. In a clearing up here a crew of fit-looking guides are unloading bikes and safety equipment whilst we stand around waiting to be told what to do next. This turns out to be a cycling proficiency test to prove we're not going to die. The test involves each person in turn accelerating, jumping over a small log and then sharply braking before falling off the side of the mountain. When my turn comes I do my best, but the instructor has his doubts about my technique and tells me to be extra careful.

The descent doesn't look too bad, in fact in places it's even uphill. I have to relearn how to ride a bike, with my centre of gravity pushed well behind the saddle, and mainly using just the rear brake. I have my first major accident in under 20 minutes. It's not about speed, as I'm not going fast, just trying to manoeuvre through the trees in the steeply sloping damp soil of the jungle floor. In fact, if I had been going faster I might not have crashed at all. Starting to wobble and losing balance, I touch the front brake, which results in my being thrown over the handlebars and into the mud, face first. A second or two later the bike lands on top of my head. Most of the group think I'll be going to hospital in an ambulance, should one be able to reach us, but what actually happens is almost miraculous. Someone lifts the bike off me, I sit up, brush the soil off and stand up. The helmet, knee and ankle pads have prevented any significant damage other than to my pride. I have two more crashes, but none as dramatic as the first. Maybe I'm learning how to fall? By the time we reach the lake at the base of the mountain later in the afternoon, my body is shot to pieces and I'm happy to spot the truck that's going to take us back into town. I haven't won any prizes, but it's been a good mental lesson to push my limits and try new things. My friends in the bar are pretty impressed to see me stagger in later that evening.

The next day I start my course at the cooking school, something that turns out to be huge fun and less likely to kill me than mountain biking, although it does involve sharp knives, powerful flames and boiling oil. And then there's the chilli, those harmless-looking little red and green peppers. Have you ever accidentally burned a chilli in a wok? It's like a chemical weapon, reducing everyone in the kitchen to coughs and splutters. And failing to remember to wash my hands after handling the little monsters results in significant pain when I scratch my nose or eyes without thinking.

The regimented routine of the school is fun, making me enjoy the moment rather than thinking about other things. Each morning we head to the market first, where I am given a shopping list of ingredients to purchase for today's dishes. To my Western eyes a lot of vegetables look very similar, and it's fortunate that the stallholders are used to helping farangs like me find the right produce.

This could have been a karate school, but instead of white pyjamas we wear blue and brown aprons. Speed, efficiency, detail and passion are the watchwords in our culinary dojo. Pon, the head chef, effortlessly demonstrates how to cook a set of three or four dishes, then dismisses us to go and make them at our cooking stations. The more days I spend there, the prouder I become of my improving techniques. I love the little details that make an average dish look like a gourmet one. Hand-carved carrots made to look like leaves, tomatoes cut to resemble roses, microscopically chiffonaded lime leaves and little dollops of coconut milk all earn us extra points. Pon walks round offering help and encouragement. His wisest words to me are 'Keep stirring, keep smiling, Matthew.' That's really a good moral guideline for

Elephant Man

life. Towards the end of the week I'm promoted to the position of Pon's assistant for the cooking demonstrations. In karate school I might have been awarded a different coloured belt, but my apron here remains the same colour, just a bit more stained from making fifty different sorts of curry. Being the demonstration assistant involves standing at the front of the class and doing a lot of stirring whilst jokes are made at my expense, but I love it. My only regret is not getting to cook my own railway rice.

My bar has the usual mix of backpackers, tourists after free internet and expats meeting up in the evenings. But I wonder if it might have a darker side too. My suspicions grow about the occupation of a few of the shadier characters. I have read in the press that somewhere nearby there is – or had been – a CIA black site. An out-of-the-way facility to process and interrogate people away from the legislative rights of prisoners held in the United States. Perhaps my imagination is running away, but I get to know a man who is always on his mobile phone with an earpiece plugged in. I won't tell you his real name, so let's call him Dave. One evening Dave has his laptop open on the bar and asks me what I think of his profile on a well-known professional recruitment website. It makes for interesting reading. Whilst he finishes a call in a language that I don't recognise – it certainly isn't

Thai – I think about what to say. I have no comments on his skills or experience, as they are very clear. My only suggestion is that I think he should mention who his current employer is at the top of his profile, to which he responds that he has been advised not to mention them. I never really get to know Dave. Most of his evenings are spent on the phone chain-smoking cigarettes outside the bar. I'm reminded of that line in the film *Apocalypse Now* when the colonel is interviewing Captain Willard for the big mission. Willard's reply to questioning about his CV is, 'Sir, I am unaware of any such activity or operation, nor would I be disposed to discuss an operation if it did in fact exist, Sir'. After Dave has told me what his next mission is going to be, if what he says is true, that's probably for the best.

I did have one military operation of my own in mind whilst I was staying in Chiang Mai. I'd heard about a collection of aircraft in a hangar on the base of Wing 41 of the Royal Thai Air Force. It's called Tango Squadron. The only problem is getting to it, as it's not open to the public most of the time. Amongst the collection of planes is the C-47 which Vice Admiral Mountbatten used as his private transport when he was Supreme Commander of the Allied Forces in South East Asia during the Second World War. It's a pretty iconic type of plane – you might know it as a

Elephant Man

Dakota. Getting hold of the right person to enquire about a visit didn't get me anywhere, so I tried a long shot and contacted the British Embassy in Bangkok. This worked like a dream, and with the help of Ben Svasti Thomson, the Honorary Consul in Chiang Mai, I find myself on an international inspection visit a few days later. Ben introduces me to the other diplomats as 'a guest of the embassy', which sounds a bit James Bond. The decaying Dakota, now painted in the colours of the Royal Thai Air Force, sits forlornly outside the hanger on the apron of the runway. The base shares the runway with the main airport so I am given a simple health and safety brief – don't cross the yellow line – which I forget in about five seconds in my excitement to get a closer look at the plane. An air force NCO has to steer me away from a passing Boeing 737 taxiing for take-off. The visit ends with a case of cold beer: excellent diplomacy in action. It sounds like there might be an international attempt to preserve the plane.

Just across the street from the place I am staying there is a shop selling painted elephants. There are lots of them in Chiang Mai; it's a social enterprise business supporting elephant welfare. I pop in most days to have a look around and a chat with Aoi, the lady who manages the shop. The story is a touching one. A Dutchman met a baby elephant called Mosha, who had been injured by a landmine close to the Burmese border. Together with his son, he set up a business to spread the message and put money back into vitally needed support. The business is now worldwide, and you can find their highly distinctive painted elephants on display at events in cities all over the world.

Each day I think about buying one, but can't decide which one of the designs I like the most. When I eventually choose one Aoi has a conversation with it as if it were a real elephant. 'Bye bye, you go to England now,' she whispers to it. She tells me that she is sad to say goodbye to this elephant, but happy for me. I now worry that my elephant might be lonely without the other elephants in the shop for company, so I buy another elephant as a companion. I'll just have to find another bag to transport them. But Aoi solves that problem. When I walk past and wave the following day, she rushes out to meet me. She asks me how the elephants are and holds up a nice bag that she has found for me. To say I'm touched is an understatement.

I decide that I could quite comfortably live in Chiang Mai for all sorts of reasons, but I need to move on. The day I'm due to take the sleeper back to Bangkok I visit my local 7/11 to buy some ice for the cold box. Finding a 7/11 in Thailand is not hard. It's a bit like the old adage that everyone lives within a few feet of a rat. There is a 7/11 on nearly every street in every town in the kingdom. Buying a beer with some ice proves much harder, though. Beer is only on sale at certain times of the day, and if it's a religious holiday it's not officially on sale at all. But I time my visit perfectly; the roller blinds are up on the beer fridge. Next comes the ice. They have an ice machine for adding ice to soft drinks, and my plan is to fill a few bags for my coolbox. Filling the first one goes well, but just as I'm perfecting my technique the machine jams and won't stop dispensing shards of ice out of its funnel and in every direction. The floor around me is quickly becoming an ice rink. The staff behind the till decide to summon their manager, who arrives on the scene to fix the machine and supervise the mop-up operation.

Round at the station, just like I found in Nong Khai, there are two trains departing for Bangkok this evening within an hour of each other. Unlike at Nong Khai, though, the stationmaster has thoughtfully provided some mobile signage to direct passengers to the right train. These look great, as there is something a bit Oriental Express about the form of their metalwork and the arrows pointing to the platform. All that's missing is a band and a red carpet. The idea isn't as crazy as it might sound. Trains with names are great for tourism. I'd love to be boarding the Elephant Train or the Jungle Express this evening.

The crew of the SE14, the first train to depart, gather for their briefing at the end of Platform 2. I decide to join in, and stand by the bell behind the officer leading the parade. The staff are lined up, everyone from the cleaning team to the guards and engineers. I wish I could understand more Thai, as I'd like to know what's being said. In my head it's 'Right, team, let's get those beds made with proper hospital corners, be nice to the farangs, and keep those boots shined.' The crew look highly motivated, so whatever his words are, they are working. The parade is soon over and they board the train.

Have you ever experienced that inexplicable human condition where you have a fixation on doing something you know is not a good idea, but you just can't stop yourself? I'm looking at the bell and feel it's screaming 'ring me'. The stationmaster takes a look at me and the bell. He has read my mind. The look on his face is, 'please don't ring the bell; that's my job'. I'm relieved when he does eventually ring it and the spell is broken. Train 14 pulls out of the station, gathering momentum, leaving behind just my train, the newer SE10, on an adjacent platform.

Elephant Man

It's a long walk down to Carriage Number 2 at the front of the train. The locomotive has already been hooked up, but there is not much activity yet. Once I have stowed my belongings I hang out on the platform trying to take some arty photographs. There are a couple of problems with this. Firstly, this makes you look like a total tourist, and secondly, as the position of the train and the platform are pretty much fixed, all my pictures of trains in stations end up looking the same. But, ready to push my artistic boundaries today, I have a new bit of kit that I picked up at a camera store in Bangkok. It's a selfie stick, which I know sounds embarrassing, but this one also works as a tripod with a remote control, which means that I can hopefully capture some fresh perspectives on platform life. As I set up my tripod a man in brightly coloured running gear strides past, down the platform, across the tracks and back along the other platform. Another recreational activity to add to a list of things to do at a Thai railway station.

Back on board I continue my education in the world of Asian crisps; I have a bag of a spicy Korean snack to try this evening that is described as 'extreme' on the packet. It came from the top shelf in 7/11, which I assume is a precaution to prevent small people from accidentally purchasing something deadly hot. My eyes water before I wash them down with a cold beverage from my minibar.

It's going to be a busy day tomorrow, so once darkness descends I ask the attendant to make up my bed. With this quickly done I lock the door and turn out the lights. Just the glow of the controls and the flashing of things whizzing past outside. I've always liked the feeling of being cocooned in my own private capsule. I get to control the lighting, the air conditioning, and organise my own living space. I think the more you travel on sleeper trains the better sleep becomes; the sounds and the movements are soporific.

Chapter Eleven
Trainspotting

I'm awake before my alarm goes off. It's the alarm clock phenomenon. My internal rhythms and hormones somehow know what time my alarm is set for and I open my eyes just before it rings. The first thing I do is to flick on the monitor screen to discover our progress. We are about 40 minutes behind schedule and I've got a text from Richard telling me to get a move on, the reason being that we have a meeting, which can't be delayed, with someone from the SRT. My plan had been to get to my hotel to drop my bags, change clothes and have some strong coffee before heading back to Hua Lamphong, but I don't have time for that now. Plan B is a shower on the train and to drop my bags off, if I have time to do so, at my hotel. This plan would have been much easier if the station had not closed down its left luggage facility.

If sleeping on a moving train feels unusual, taking a shower on one feels really strange. The shower on this train turns out to be powerful, with an initial dribble of cold water becoming jets of steaming hot water once it gets going. I discover that the secret to success here is to keep a wide stance with my feet and swivel my hips in order to remain stable as the carriage sways from side to side. I imagine this to be like balancing on a surfboard, but as I have never managed to stand up on a surfboard I can't be sure. Drying off with the tiny towel provided, I emerge a few minutes later with a smile on my face and feeling considerably fresher.

I haven't thought about what I might need to wear for a meeting, so I have to improvise from my bags. The best that I can come up with are my tartan trousers and a linen shirt made for me by My Sunny, a rather good Burmese tailor that I came across in Chiang Mai. I hope this will pass for Thai business casual. I get my bags down to the doors of the carriage before we arrive, then I pop back to my room to collect the elephants, which don't yet have names. As soon as we arrive at the platform the carriage attendant senses my urgency, and helps me get the bags down and I'm off before most people realise we have arrived.

I have by now become a master in the taxi operation at Hua Lamphong. Exit round the side of the platforms, keep looking straight ahead and ignore the people asking you if you need a taxi. Of course you *do* want a taxi, but that isn't their business. Then pass a narrow entrance at the kerbside to find the official rank, which makes it easy to deal directly with the driver at the front of the queue, something which the touts can do nothing about. The boot of my taxi this morning isn't big enough for my big bag, so I give up and sit next to it in the back seat. Why do they make bags that don't fit in taxi boots, or taxi boots not big enough for bags?

The plan works out better than I had hoped, and I'm back at Bangkok Station with enough time for some much-needed caffeine before our meeting. The coffee shops are on a mezzanine level inside the main hall, and offer a great view down onto the floor below. Richard joins me here and we find a table with a view. Almost straight away he points down to someone in the crowd below. 'I think that's him,' he says. For someone we have never met before he must have some special identification skills. 'How do you know?' I ask him. Richard waves down to the group. 'He's got an entourage, and they've come in through the front doors'. The front doors are usually locked here, and I'm not sure why. We finish our breakfast and head down to the magic doors, which are now being supervised by a couple of station guards. We've clearly been identified, as one of them reports our arrival on his walkie-talkie as we approach, and the other unlocks the gate and gestures for us to step through.

At the front of the station is a very familiar Bangkok landmark, the fountain with the elephant statue and behind it, across Rama IV Road, is the site of the original Hua Lamphong Station which served the private Paknam Railway Line between 1893 and 1960. There is currently more naming confusion here. Bangkok Railway Station is not only known as Hua Lamphong, but also Krung Thep,[14] the Thai name for the city, and underneath the road here is the MRT station of the same name. One thing that most people don't know is that also under the fountain was an air raid shelter in the Second World War. There is no visible way in, but I wonder if there might be some perfectly preserved history left underground.

Richard and I are escorted round to the small doorway that is the entrance to a railway museum,

---

[14] City of Angels

and inside we find ourselves in a small room dripping with railway memorabilia. Every possible space is taken with tickets, crockery, silverware, clocks, signalling equipment and signage. Richard speaks good Thai, and helps with the introductions. I'm impressed that a former Deputy Governor of the State Railway of Thailand has taken time out of his busy schedule to meet with us on a Saturday morning. Dr Siriphong Preutthipan is the President of the Thai Railway Foundation, and has kindly agreed to give us a history lesson before showing us around. I take this is a great opportunity to learn and reflect upon the origins of Thailand's railway. Dr Siriphong has some seriously detailed notes to refer to, and tells us the story.

In the 1880s several private railway tenders were awarded, but nothing was actually built until the construction of the 13-mile-long narrow-gauge Paknam Railway Line, which opened in 1893. Then in 1897 the Royal State Railways of Siam opened its first railway line, massively shortening the travel time between Bangkok and Ayutthaya. With the help of German, British and Dutch locomotives a network was developed, weaving around the politics of international frontiers and intervening wars. After the Second World War the Royal Railway Department became the State Railway of Thailand which, with World Bank loans, purchased locomotives: 142 from the Allies, 74 from Japan and 68 from the United States. More rolling stock was also purchased from Japan and Switzerland. Several new lines were built in the 1950s, when rail was still the prime method of transportation. Sleeper trains arrived in the 1960s, and by the late 1970s the steam locomotives were mostly replaced by diesel engines.

I make a lot of notes whilst Richard asks increasingly detailed questions. I have three points in my notebook for further investigation:

-   a railway perhaps inspired by a Victorian model trainset.

-   swings between international ambitions and domestic role over time.

-   no sleeper trains before the 1960s – railway hotels.

Once our history class is complete Dr Siriphong opens up some of the wooden cases that line the walls, allowing us to handle objects that would be irreplaceable if they were to be damaged. I also find a vintage platform bell in the corner, and this time cannot resist having a go at ringing it. This turns out not to be as easy as it looks. I try to sound the departure ring with long pauses in between dings,

Trainspotting

but my technique needs considerable work as I end up double-clanging each ding.

If you follow the signs to the toilets in the main station concourse at Hua Lamphong you will find a set of secret stairs. They are not invisible like Platform 9¾ at London's Kings Cross, but in plain sight, cordoned off by metal shutters that Dr Siriphong opens up for us. The double staircase with wrought-iron rails and tiled walls leads upstairs to a hidden world. The secret is revealed on the first floor, where they open onto a foyer that was once the reception of the Ratchathani Railway Hotel, part of a small chain of railway hotels directly owned by the SRT along with other properties in Chiang Mai, Hua Hin and Hat Yai. The place takes you back to an age of the railway grand tour. On one side of the corridor along the length of the station are windows looking out over the platforms and on the other side are doorways into the guest rooms. I notice that they each have a little hatch low down in the wall, perhaps to serve breakfast in the room or empty a chamber pot. I have a fantasy of staying in a hotel like this, one where you can wake up in the morning and take breakfast in bed with the sound of the steam trains readying to take you to your destination. But I'm being a bit unrealistically Kiplingesque, as I am thinking of porters with trolleys, pith helmets and of course an ironed copy of the daily newspaper.

The future of the station building is uncertain. The rumour is that it might once again be turned into a hotel and hold a bigger museum. Steam engines might even stand on the tracks. I hope so, as once heritage like this is gone you can't get it back. I have also heard that Thailand will also soon have a new railway-themed hotel at Khao Yai, proof of concept that heritage railway tourism will grow in the future. Guests will be able to stay in upcycled railway carriages in a stunning setting. Both projects will undoubtedly be amazing places for train enthusiasts in the future.

After lunch we take a ride out to Makkasan, the original railway depot on the Eastern Line. The entrance to the yard is very close to where I thought I'd found the location of the *Combat Rock* album cover on my journey to Pattaya a few weeks ago. If life on the rails in Thailand were a religion this place would be its most important temple. Originally built in 1897 and then rebuilt after being heavily bombed by the Allies in the Second World War, it is still today the main repair yard for the country's rolling stock. We get ushered in through security at the main gate, where we are greeted by the sight of a train graveyard. An eclectic mix of locomotives are lined up on a siding from the main tracks from the nearby station. Some are freshly painted, others totally rusted away and taken over by creepers. This is a place not just for the repair of everyday carriages, but also to maintain and store historic trains – even the royal carriages are hidden away here. I'm kept busy here with my book of steam locomotive numbers. Richard and I are allowed to play with the trains here as much as we like. Climbing up and into some of the cabs is more challenging than I expected. It's all about technique with the footholds and handrails. But our playtime abruptly ends when the heavens open, another of those Bangkok afternoon storms. There's no point in fighting nature, so we find some shelter and Dr Siriphong breaks out a bag of mangosteens to eat whilst we chat about railways until it's time to go home. As a memento of the day, he presents us each with a china plate depicting King Rama V and a steam engine. I only hope that it survives the rest of my journey in one piece.

Bang Sue Junction

Chapter Twelve
The Delicate Sound of Thunder

It's time to prepare for my next adventure. The streets of Bang Rak have some amazing places to shop. Not the mall experience that dominates the aspirations of upwardly mobile Bangkok shoppers, but the unfussy concrete shop houses that spill out onto the streets with awnings overhead, leaving the passers-by on the pavements of busy roads with just a couple of feet to squeeze past. My personal favourite are the shops that sell kitchenware; I can't walk past one without having a look around. I'm in a jungle of dangling woks, meat cleavers, bamboo baskets, bird cages and industrial quantities of brightly coloured Tupperware. I have to move on

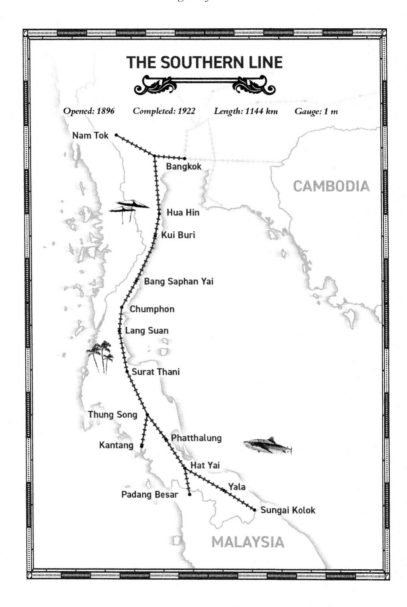

The Delicate Sound of Thunder

before I get carried away. I find some suitable but boring snacks at my local 7/11, and also pick up some flowers from a shop next door. I'm going to give them to workers on the train, in case they don't like my jelly babies.

It's a short trip to Hua Lamphong in a taxi today. My Chinese driver speaks no English, but impresses me with his knowledge of the backstreet shortcuts that take half the time of the satnav recommendations on the main roads. He even gets an extra point for using a car park as a jam-busting cut-through. One of the sad things about the station these days is that all the interesting food vendors have moved out. They have left partly because of Covid and partly because no one has told them that, contrary to popular belief, the station may actually be running for years to come. The newspapers say that the new Central Terminal will take over this year, but that simply can't happen for all sorts of technical reasons. This means that today my choices are limited to the coffee shops and the dreaded plastic-wrapped Asian sandwich. If you've not had one you've not missed anything: two pieces of nearly stale white bread with the crusts cut off and a depressing filling of processed ham or cheese, margarine optional, and garnished with limp lettuce on high days and holidays.

Today I'm heading south, out past Thonburi, and then down the Southern Line as far as Hat Yai Junction. I've been looking forward to this journey both for its distance and for the change of scenery. The Southern Line is actually made up of seven branch lines, covering destinations in the west and south of the kingdom. First opened in 1903, its tracks extend over 1400 km, terminating in Su-ngai Kolok at the Malaysian land border. Another branch heads to the main rail frontier at Padang Besar, the route of the international train that has headed into Malaysia and on to Singapore since 1918. My 1928 *Guide to Bangkok* says, 'Travellers will find every comfort and convenience on the express trains between Penang and Bangkok. The first class Day and Night coaches used in this service are arranged in compartments. Each compartment contains two berths arranged somewhat like the Pullman compartment car used in the United States.'

Originally this line was separate from the rest of the network, running into Thonburi Station as its terminus. That's the station that also serves the line up to Nam Tok which I travelled on a few weeks ago. In 1927 the construction of an extension line over the Chao Phraya River in Bangkok finally connected everything up, and now trains can run out of Hua Lamphong. It confuses me slightly that all the best-timed trains to Nam Tok still run out

The Delicate Sound of Thunder

of Thonburi, though. The SRT computer system has its own view of Thonburi. If you buy a ticket there it prints the word 'defunct' after the station name. I have no idea why, but that must be rum news if you work there.

Today there are three significant problems with my journey. Firstly, that there are currently no trains crossing the frontier to Malaysia via Padang Besar. The border is closed. The second is that the tracks in the south are suffering from serious flooding at the moment, and many trains are cancelled or delayed by as much as a day. The third is that on the east side of the peninsula, the route down to Su-ngai Kolok is subject to the risk of terrorist attacks from local separatist insurgents, drug cartels, oil smugglers and even pirates. In fact, the train that travels south of Hat Yai on the line to Su-ngai Kolok is known by some as the Insurgency Express. It has been attacked or bombed more than 100 times since 2004, making it one of the most dangerous railway lines in the world. But life goes on, and the trains still run – they just have soldiers on board, brandishing assault rifles. Several trains have recently been derailed by bombings. I read about one incident last year; Train 452 running was attacked near Pattani, but miraculously no one was killed. The driver had the courage to keep the train moving to the next station after the explosion, taking its 300 passengers to relative safety.

As the Foreign Office have put this area on their red 'advise against all travel' list, I'm going to finish my trip at Hat Yai Junction. You may well have heard of Hat Yai without realising why. If you have ever sat in the back of a wide-bodied aircraft, bored by the selection of inflight entertainment and switched on the interactive map, Hat Yai always shows up on planes cruising between the Andaman Sea and the Gulf of Thailand. Above the clouds, I have often wondered what sort of place is beneath me. Now it's time to find out.

Special Express 31 is due to depart Hua Lamphong at 12.30, and is scheduled to arrive in Hat Yai at 07.25 tomorrow morning. But with all the rain, that could be optimistic. I'm in no hurry, though. It's the usual procedure here today. Finishing my coffee, I head down and cross the hall, pass under the painting of the King and out onto the platform where the train is waiting for me. At the door I meet my attendant, Thanin, who shows me to my room. He's super friendly, and makes me feel very welcome. If I ran a railway I would pay a bonus for staff to be friendly, as it transforms the experience of taking a train. I once spent some time on the rails in Japan and could not

The Delicate Sound of Thunder

believe the politeness and etiquette of the railway workers. I had the similar experience, albeit a bit patchy, in the United States. It gave me the idea of a reality television show where railway workers do a job swap with those working in other countries. It might make interesting viewing.

I don't hear the bell announcing our imminent departure, but it must be being rung somewhere by the stationmaster responsible for departing trains. My carriage is very busy today. I've noticed that sleepers with rooms are popular with families, as you can squeeze in as many kids in as you like for the same price. The kids are stopping to stare at me every time they pass by, and I have run out of jelly babies, so eventually I have to pull the door shut to get some peace. Here in my own room I can have as much or as little interaction with the other passengers as I like. From my comfy seat next to the window I pull down the armrest and pop the table beneath the window up so that I can make some notes. People often ask me if I get bored on long-distance trains, and my answer is that I just don't have time to. I'm always content with what I'm doing. Most of the time I would like the journey to be longer.

Later in the afternoon I observe a change in the weather, and before long we encounter another of those perfect storms. Stair rods of water batter my

Bang Sue Junction

window, making it hard to see much of the outside world. When we pull into a small town at about 6pm, polystyrene boxes of food materialise in the carriage – fried chicken, spicy rice and some vegetables that I don't recognise. I miss the dining car, but this is still fun, a private picnic in my own room. It reminds me somewhat of a school packed lunch, but without the bruised apple and the out-of-date pork pie.

After dinner Thanin appears and offers to make my bed, so I step out into the corridor to give him space. If you were going to give someone marks for bed making, Thanin is a definite ten out of ten. He manages to use friction under the bed to hold and stretch the sheets into a perfectly flat and wrinkle-free bed. I wonder if his bed-making skills have been acquired in the military, but I don't ask. Instead I just give him a thankful *wai* and wish him a good night.

In the night we bump along through the rains, and I sleep through our stops at Hua Hin and later at Surat Thani. This is the jumping-off point for travellers headed to the islands in the Gulf of Thailand or over to Phuket in the Andaman Sea. When a misty dawn arrives, I open my curtains and see palm trees, lush green paddy fields and limestone outcrops towering above the train. Buffalo graze on the vegetation with white storks

The Delicate Sound of Thunder

sitting contentedly on their backs. Alongside the track there is water everywhere, and the roads have become lakes almost reaching the height of the rails. The weather in these parts is predictable at this time of the year, with heavy rain and thunderstorms forecast for several weeks to come. If I lived here I would definitely invest in a good kayak.

By the time Special Express 31 arrives at Hat Yai Junction we have made up some time but are still running 3 hours late. It's stopped raining, leaving behind an overcast and crushingly humid morning. Platform 1 is busy with vendors' stalls and railway staff unloading bags, boxes of post and even motorbikes. I didn't realise before this trip that the railway also acts as a mini-postal service, conveying packages of all shapes and sizes to stations across the country. By the time I have wandered to the front of the train for the obligatory photo of the station sign and a wave to the driver, most of the passengers have left. Unusually for Thailand, there is an underpass to the other platform and a gateway exit bypassing the station offices. A man guarding the gate opens it up to let me out. This is all part of the higher level of security that now covers the Southern Line from here as far as the border. There have been no bombings in Hat Yai Station since 2001, and it's obviously the plan to keep it that way. The city itself, though, has not been so lucky, with several bombings, drive-by shootings and machete attacks in recent years.

I'm hungry, but before I can seek sustenance I'm drawn towards some railway history. There is an official railway hotel here right outside the station. It looks pretty basic, but this is still part of the railway story of Thailand. When the cross-border line was connected up in 1918, two trains per week travelled through to Malaya, a journey of around 60 hours if everything was running well. In the early days there were few sleeper services, so as an addition to homestays the Royal State Railways of Siam built several hotels along the line for passengers to stay overnight, breaking up their journeys. As well as the one here, there is also a much larger hotel in Hua Hin. The SRT still owns these properties and leases them to hotel operators.

A few years ago, I travelled south all the way to Singapore. I passed through both Hua Hin and Hat Yai, and onward to the border crossing at Pandang Besar. The train was then known as the International Express, Thailand's only cross-border service. It was supposed to take me all the way to Butterworth. I'm not sure what went wrong, but we pulled into the frontier station with

The Delicate Sound of Thunder

a lot of squealing underneath our carriage, which was declared unserviceable and uncoupled from the rest of the train. I'm pleased this happened after breakfast, as it would have been rather confusing in the middle of the night. But it turned out that we had to get off the train here anyway. If the purpose of a through train is to make international travel smoother, no one had told the officials at Pandang Besar. Everyone had to process immigration and customs in an office on the platform before rejoining the train. The officials were pretty thorough, and I soon found out why, when the replacement carriage they put me in was full of currency traders and cigarette smugglers. By lunchtime we arrived in Butterworth and I took the short ferry ride across the bright blue sea to Penang, where I stayed briefly at the wonderful Eastern and Oriental Hotel in Georgetown. Opened by the Sarkis brothers in 1889 it was billed as the premier hotel east of the Suez, providing its guests with every luxury. It had the sort of bar where you could easily imagine yourself sitting next to fellow guests like Rudyard Kipling, Noël Coward and Somerset Maugham en route by train from Bangkok to Singapore, where the Sarkis brothers had also recently opened a new hotel called Raffles.

The Train Hotel in Hat Yai has none of the grandeur and opulence of the work of the Sarkis brothers. When the junction was built the city didn't exist, so a hotel was needed here. The current station isn't the original one, which was abandoned as it was prone to flooding. Given the weather today, I'm not at all surprised. It isn't a pretty station by Thai standards and the hotel is not much more than a concrete block. Whilst this might be a tad depressing, at the front of the hotel I find Locomotive Number 32, a cute-looking little Japanese steam engine dating back to 1949.

Hat Yai is of course no longer a village. More than 400,000 people live here today, with a curious mix of ethnicity, including large numbers of Thai Chinese and Thai Malay people. As you walk across town this is immediately obvious. There are mosques as well as temples here, and ornate Chinese shops can still be found behind the concrete city blocks. I can't sense any danger here. Some places in the world make me feel uncomfortable, but life on the streets here this morning seems calm and friendly. I find a restaurant a couple of blocks away with chefs busy cooking in an open kitchen at the street front. I try my best to blend in — but fat chance, everyone is looking at me. I think that they want to know what I'm going to order. The menu is in a little plastic case on the table, with versions in Thai and Chinese, and the people at the next table help me to translate it. I opt for the fried spicy pork and

The Delicate Sound of Thunder

some green tea. Spicy turns out to be a gross under-description. To begin with I just can't stop sneezing from the vapour rising from the red-hot sizzling skillet delivered to my table. I'm the centre of entertainment for a few minutes, but eventually get nods of approval as I polish it off. I can relax here for a while, and sip my tea watching the chefs set fire to all sorts of dishes.

It's not too hard to navigate around Hat Yai. Unlike most Thai cities it's designed in the style of a new town with a grid of wide blocks and traffic lights. I find the place I'm staying at not too far away. It is mildly funky, both outside and in, the architect clearly influenced by the sort of glass-fronted hotels that you now find in most European cities. The receptionist at the desk is protected by a massive plastic screen with various slots carved in it for passing through cash, keys and paperwork. It wouldn't be Asia if various notices didn't start multiplying on its flat surface, and I read a variety of warnings ranging from breakfast etiquette through to the fines for theft of items from the room. This must be a crime hotspot, as although I have already paid for a room I have to leave a large cash deposit, hopefully to be returned when I check out.

It's the usual story. My room won't be ready for several hours, so I have time to visit nearby

Songkhla, the provincial capital on the coast, around 15 miles (24 km) away. Up until 1978 you could take a train there, and although it still has the original station at the end of the line, the car is now king and a short motorway connects the two cities. Reception summon a taxi for me and the young man who arrives dressed in an ill-fitting dark suit looks like he might be a safe driver, but his appearance is deceptive. I decline his request to pay upfront and we set off in financial stalemate. He wastes no time on the journey, with every stationary moment filled with personal grooming. He cuts his nails at the first few sets of red lights. I next open my eyes, we are crawling along the coast road. My driver squints into the wing mirror and then decides to put his glasses on.

Songkhla turns out to be pretty sleepy. The car park at the beach is full of street vendors without any customers. Their stalls are packed with inflatable animals, candyfloss and toys. Dark-skinned cowboys dressed in Milky Bar Kid outfits parade ponies, offering rides to just a handful of holidaymakers. The rail border to Malaysia might be closed, but you can still drive across. This area feels like a different country to the rest of Thailand, and that's part of the problem, fuelling several separatist movements.

The Delicate Sound of Thunder

I could get to quite like life in Hat Yai. Every modern convenience and a great jumping-off point in southern Thailand for all sorts of adventures. But when I told people back in Bangkok that I was headed to Hat Yai next, the first thing they all mentioned without exception was the fried chicken. I set off to a place downtown where I have been told that I'll find the very best fried chicken in the whole of Thailand. Ducking under the awnings outside the concrete-walled market, I smell it before I see it: lots of stalls selling only chicken. I'm sure the locals each have their favourite chef, but I have to take a chance and choose the first stall where its owner looks pleased to see me. Looking at her assembly area and deep-frying setup, I see she has an impressive array of metal pots full of special, possibly secret, ingredients. 'You wan chi-een?' she asks. I give up on my schoolboy Thai, and give her a thumbs-up. 'Hat Yai fried chicken, please,' I say, as though there is any possibility that she might be going to make me some Hua Hin or Chiang Mai fried chicken. A couple of poultry-shaped objects with contorted joints are exhumed from the bubbling oil, drained and set on a banana leaf. Then the magic happens, the crispy fried shallots and a dipping sauce are added, along with some plain rice. I perch on a plastic stool next to the cooking area and breathe in the aroma from the plate in front of me. One bite of the thin crispy crust takes me to a new level of Thai food heaven. The woman smiles when she notices that she has a new happy customer. '*Aroy mak mak,*' I tell her – 'it's delicious'. It's so good that I dream about it in my lumpy hotel bed that night.

I'm up early the next morning in case there is going to be any problem with my security deposit. Reception radio up to housekeeping who carry out a thorough search of my room against a detailed inventory. The walkie-talkie crackles and they report back. I'm all clear. The TV is still there, and I haven't stolen the toilet roll holder either. Thinking about it, I'm lucky to have a toilet roll holder in the first place. My deposit is returned and I'm free to go about my day without suspicion of any criminal activity.

On the way to the railway station I discover a dim sum restaurant in a row of brightly coloured Chinese shop houses on a back street. In a city mainly made up of concrete blocks, this looks amazing and ideal for a pre-train brunch. I could spend the day in a place like this. Freshly steamed dumplings and jasmine tea until I can eat no more. I like nearly all types of dumplings, except any involving feet, owing to a bad experience in the Philippines a few years ago; I went to a friend's birthday party in Cebu, where the buffet turned out to be entirely made up of chicken's feet, cooked in several different ways. Anyway, my brunch today is thankfully a foot-free feast. I'm puzzled by a picture frame on the wall above my table. It has a film poster I can't read, and a plaque from the side of Carriage Number 6 of the Bangkok–Hat Yai Express. The poster is one of those colourful drawings that film posters used to feature. In the background men fight with martial arts gear and handguns, and at the front of the poster a woman wearing a wide-brimmed straw hat looks in control of the situation, whatever the situation actually is. Carriage Number 6 appears to be a central part of the plot.

The news at the station isn't good for trains, but much better for water buffalo and ducks; all trains are delayed by flooding on the line. No one seems very certain by exactly how much, and I can't build any confidence that the train is even going to run today. I'm a bit confused; as this is the starting point on the timetable the train should be here, but my suspicion is that it has got stuck in floods coming south. I'd like to wait for it, but I have business in Bangkok tomorrow, so there is little option but for Plan B. I'll have to fly. It's not like this is against my religion, but I had hoped to be just travelling on the rails. On the plus side, I will now be back in Bangkok in time for a cold beer in

Jack's Bar before the sun sets. I'm seduced by this thought and get a ride out to the airport.

To quote Colonel Hannibal Smith from the A-Team TV series, 'I love it when a plan comes together.' I book a flight on my phone and stroll into the terminal with an hour to spare like it was all planned weeks ago. I'm old enough to remember the days of paper tickets, travel agents and fax machines. This would have been a big problem to sort out back then. The airport feels alien after some time on the rails, but once on the plane, everything is rather cramped but pleasant enough. As I'm getting off the crew even give me a packed lunch — current rules prevent it from being served in the air. I've missed the chance to think and write on the train, but I'll soon catch up.

Chapter Thirteen
The Railway People

I'm staying at a hotel on the other side of the river for a couple of nights. You might have heard about it for all the wrong reasons. It's the Bangkok Hilton. I have always felt for whoever was the Hilton brand manager in 1989, and I have tried to imagine the moment when they learned the name for a new Australian television mini-series. *The Bangkok Hilton*, starring Nicole Kidman and Denholm Elliot, told a story of heroin trafficking and the brutality of the Thai prison system. It can't have been good for either the hotel or for tourism to Thailand in general at the time. Even more strangely, whilst much of the series was filmed in Australia, some parts were even filmed in Bangkok

Bang Sue Junction

— and at another hotel which is not connected with the Hilton brand. It must have been an interesting location negotiation.

The roof of the hotel has a bar with views across the city. I enjoy a frosty beer and try not to think about its price. The peanuts are free, though, but only because they make you want to drink more. All the clichés of the setting sun play out here as the cocktail set arrive to take Instagram photos of their mostly imaginary jetset lifestyles. But I'm more excited by one aspect of the view. I have a direct line of sight down to Hua Lamphong Station from up here on the 32nd floor. The hotel would be ideally suited for rail passengers if it were not for the snaking Chao Phraya River in between. It would make a great zip line ride, though. Off the top of the Hilton, over River City Shopping Mall and into the front window of Hua Lamphong itself.

My plan was to visit Bang Kwang Prison between rail trips. Its nickname is the Big Tiger, apparently because the harsh regime eats prisoners up. It's a men's prison (unlike the women's prison in the *Bangkok Hilton* television film), and it houses most of the foreigners in Thai jails, including death row inmates. I don't know why I thought it was a good idea to do this, but I had an itch that needed scratching. The process for visiting isn't

The Railway People

straightforward. First you need to speak with your embassy to find out the names of prisoners who are accepting visits, and then a prisoner needs to agree to your meeting. On arrival at the jail there is an unsurprisingly thorough search and confiscation of your belongings if you make it onto the daily visitor list. But it quickly becomes apparent that my visit won't be possible. No visitors are allowed right now, as Covid is currently rife in Thai prisons. This should be a shock to no one, given the overcrowding and generally poor conditions.

I check out the next morning and relocate to another hotel, one that I can't really afford to stay at, but I want to spend a large quantity of loyalty points that are just about to expire. After a lavish buffet breakfast, I track down Tim Russell in reception. Tim is a well-known Bangkok photographer, and he has agreed to join me on the rails today. We don't hang around, and get a taxi to our first stop, Wongwian Yai, the station at the Bangkok end of the line to Mae Klong that I visited when I was trying to reach the Dangerous Market a few weeks ago. It's another blisteringly hot day and my drab-coloured t-shirt is quickly soaked with sweat. One expat told me the secret is to wear a t-shirt under a shirt, to soak up the perspiration, but I'll just have to look sweaty and rugged today.

Other than getting some good train photos, we are here to find out more about the lives of the communities who live and work within touching distance of the railway. These are the people that I have seen from my seat on board several trains on the tracks out of Hua Lamphong. I want to understand more on why they choose to live such an apparently precarious existence.

Wongwian Yai might be small, but it's more than just a railway station. It's a social centre, a community club and a shopping centre all rolled into one. Hopping up onto the platform we take a seat on the concrete next to a happy man tending to a big hot pot. I have heard about these things. The concept is that once you start cooking you just keep it permanently going, adding things to it. Bits and pieces might have gone into the dish in 1981 or 2021, it's luck of the draw. The chef fishes out some greasy-looking noodles with indeterminate protein and offers me a plate. I pass on these, and instead gulp down a couple of litres of chilled water from his ice box.

Walking along a train track is a mad idea, and an alien concept to the average European. But it's what we are doing today. It's mad for two reasons. Firstly, that there is a chance of a horrible death from the approaching trains. At big tourist spots like Mae Klong and the Kwai bridge, the driver

The Railway People

slows right down and blows the horn a lot for the tourists, but in this part of the city they assume you know the drill and that you will spot the train before it hits you. The second reason is that it's hard work. The distance between the sleepers mean that you have to either stride like a crazy nightclub performer, or trot along taking baby steps. Where possible we stick to paths next to the line, but these can be risky too. Missing concrete slabs and uncovered gutters open up the possibility of broken ankles or a watery grave in the sewers beneath.

As we move along the side of the tracks close to the station the food vendors begin to thin out and people are now selling what look to be the contents of their homes. I suspect these people are a non-resident part of the rail community, day traders who are taking advantage of the volume of passengers commuting into the city to shift their wares. I eye up the array of weird trinkets and kids' toys, and I'm just about to ask the price of a beaten-up Buzz Lightyear action doll when Tim encourages me to keep going. I shift between bouncy big steps and little steps in a new form of track aerobics, looking down at my feet to judge the sleepers right as we walk in the direction of the next station down the line. 'Train,' Tim says from up front, but at first I don't hear him. He then repeats the message with more urgency, and I look up to see an oncoming locomotive in the distance. I'm surprised by how fast it approaches, even though it's a slow commuter train. It is only when you are down on the tracks that you get the sense of scale and mass of a train compared to a human being. Tim is off the line before me, and he looks back to check that I've made it too. Moments later the engine trundles over the spot where I had been performing my aerobics. The good news is that there are now no further scheduled trains for two and a half hours, but I'm not taking the timetable as a guarantee. When we reach Talat Phlu I congratulate myself for saving 3 baht (7p) on the rail fare – but the water I need to consume as a result of the walk costs 20 baht. This is a proper old-school railway station. The furniture, the colours and the design are wonderful.

On the tracks from Hua Lamphong I have seen people living right next to the rails. But so far today our walk has only revealed a lighter version of this lifestyle. Things change when we arrive in Phaya Thai. At first I think we must be in the wrong place. This is a prosperous part of central Bangkok made up of leafy streets lined with coffee shops in the shade of the BTS superstructure running above. My 1928 *Guide to Bangkok* suggests that the Phya Thai Palace Hotel, located here, was the place to stay in the city: 'It is open to breezes from any quarter and free from the din and dust of the city.'

The Railway People

A deluxe suite with hall, sitting room, writing room and bathroom was 120 baht per night back then. Although it is now sadly a barracks and a hospital, the area remains upmarket. Even the 7/11 here looks like a posh one, with tall steps and a tinted glass front. But as can be the way in big Asian cities, behind a façade of modern development hides the old world, and around the other side of the block is a railway station on the Eastern Line, now dwarfed by the development of the BTS line above. I'm calling it a station, but I'm being generous; it's really just a wayside halt. There is a small station building extending into the bushes, and the platform is about a metre wide and made of uneven concrete slabs at ground level. Past this building is a ribbon-like development of houses and shacks made of wood and corrugated iron. These are the homes of the Bun Romsai community, one of several groups who settled on public land next to the rails back in the 1970s and decided to stay. Some say that these settlers once worked on the railway.

Next to the abandoned ticket office I find a timetable pasted onto the wall. I'm not sure how old it is, but it looks like some local trains might still stop here. I'm taking this possibility in when a boy on a moped squeezes past, presumably on his way home from high school. We obviously don't really belong here, but he's friendly and says hello.

Bang Sue Junction

We work our way along the platform until we find a store selling all kinds of stuff. It's the Thai equivalent of the British corner shop, but not on a corner and right next to a railway line in Bangkok. I can see stacks of soft drinks bottles, plastic pots of cooking oil and bags of rice in the dim interior. Further back there is a rudimentary kitchen, and a hammock is strung up from the roof. The shopkeeper appears from the shadows, shirtless but wearing a colourful purple sarong and a pair of well-worn flip-flops. He's pleased to see us, not in a wanting to sell us things sort of way, more just to socialise. He lives here, and so do the people on either side of him; one is a tailor and the other runs a basic post office. There are over 100 families living here, but many are leaving as the land is owned by the SRT and is now needed to build the new high-speed rail line. He tells us that they will be relocated to a nearby low-cost housing development in the next couple of years, but it's not ready yet and the developers want to move in right now…

Each trackside home has its own low-tech architectural style and is spray-painted with a house number. You might even be able to send mail to an address here. There are lots of items upcycled from household junk, and not much seems to be wasted. Food containers are converted into banks of plant pots and irrigation systems. Rocks are

The Railway People

piled up to form small walls, and cut-up oil drums are used as makeshift barbecues. The outlook from the little shop is tidy, organised and surprisingly green for the middle of the city. Nature has been allowed a ribbon of freedom along the trackside banks. My sense of meeting with the railway people is that they are well adapted to a simple life. They have jobs, but can't afford conventional rent in the heart of the city. It's sad that they are being forced to leave, but I understand they have been offered money as compensation if they don't want to move into the new housing estate.

Back at Jack's Bar, Tim and I build up a small mountain of empty bottles next to our riverside table. With the water lapping at my feet under the floorboards and the low sun reflecting off the river I'm in my happy place. Tim does the sensible thing and heads home, but I find myself still in the same seat several hours later talking to people about trains. I have become the bar's very own Forrest Gump,[15] or at least a railway version of him.

---

[15] 1994 comedy drama film based on a novel by Winston Groom

Bang Sue Junction

Chapter Fourteen
Cool Hand Matthew

Once again I'm back in my favourite Thai railway station today. My ticket has been issued to a Mr Matthew, who has a second-class reservation on the 171 Rapid train as far as Hua Hin. This train continues on southward all the way to Su-ngai Kolok, but it's a relatively short run for me today, just over 5 hours if everything runs on time.

On the way to my carriage I encounter a lady who actually has more baggage than I do. She is trying to load the complete contents of her apartment onto the train. The guards are conflicted. I think that they want to help, but can't be seen to support the transport of luggage on this scale. I lend a hand, but my thoughts are about where she is going to stow it all once she gets on board. (I came across

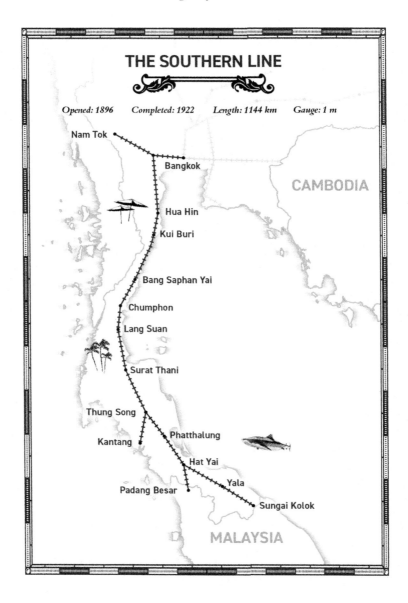

this problem in Mongolia a few years ago. Traders fill up all the compartments, including yours, with sacks of grain and giant cartons of eggs until you tell them to stop. I didn't mind until someone told me that they also smuggle booze and cigarettes, at which point I carried out a full inventory check of the locker under my bed.) I wish her well and head off down the platform to find my carriage.

I think 5 hours is a good length for a daytime journey. Longer ones tend to drag a bit, and shorter ones are not worth really settling in for. It turns out that my second-class ticket is for a seat in a sleeper coach, which during the daytime is a pretty comfortable place to be. It has pairs of bed-wide seats facing each other, alongside the windows. As no one is sitting opposite me this is like being in first class on a plane. The train also has second-class carriages with just seats, which are cheaper but have a bit less room for luggage. The general order of the cost of seats and beds on Thai trains starts with first class, a two-person sleeper in its own compartment which you can buy for sole occupancy. Next are open-plan second-class sleepers with air conditioning, then sleepers with an open window and a fan. The daytime second-class carriages have normal seats and come with either fans or air conditioning. Finally, good old third class with fans and bench seats. I love them all for different reasons. For a journey like this

Bang Sue Junction

during the daytime I'd be just as happy with a breeze coming through the window in a second or third-class carriage with fans. I have also found that a second-class sleeper can be just as nice as a first-class one, providing similar comfort but a more social experience in the open-plan. But as we trundle out into the fierce midday heat I decide that maybe it is good thing to be in an air-conditioned carriage today after all.

I hear the guard before I see him. He's playing with his empty clippers in the style of a cowboy practising drawing a trusty revolver. I'm beginning to get familiar with this part of the line. Out of the station, apartment blocks are at first right up against the edge of the tracks, slowly receding with enough space to allow railway people to establish their homes. They are larger here than at Phaya Thai, with small gardens and space to park mopeds.

It's busy here in Carriage 13, but the low density of seating allows a sense of peace until we stop at Bang Sue Junction, where all hell breaks loose. A bunch of food vendors board the train, laden with a rail-based banquet of fried rice, fresh fruit and strange-looking pastries. Some of the sellers here don't want to miss a moment of potential sales revenue, so they remain on board as the train departs before jumping off. It looks pretty dangerous to me, but they must be experienced enough to know where and when to leap. Others remain on board until the next station, just in case anyone changes their mind, or decides to have a second serving. I wish the vendors would not shout out what they are selling as they pass by every few minutes, but they are competing with each other for sales. Time for some music. At first I try listening to *Combat Rock*, but The Clash are just too aggressive for the rhythm of the rails. I shuffle through various albums until I settle on some Steely Dan, always unbeatable to lift my mood.

This carriage is an older type, one that I think was manufactured in Korea in the 1980s. Whilst it's comfy, it has none of the technological features of the latest Chinese coaches, so I'm using a map on my phone to check on our progress. The world depends on power sockets on the move these days, something that was not a consideration when these coaches were built. In this carriage it's the person at Seat 30 who controls access to the single socket. The lady sitting there today is our goddess of power. She oversees a nest of wires daisy-chained to all sorts of devices. It's an important job, and passengers approach her reverentially to join the queue to plug in. I lower my head as I pass her on the way to the toilets.

I choose one of the two doors, which is engaged, so try the opposite one. Stuck to the door is a cartoon illustration of two happy SRT workers and the caption – 'Smelly? Tell me!' There is even a QR code. It must have been a fun creative session in the advertising agency when they came up with that one. The door is a bit stiff, but once I'm sure the toilet is not occupied I manage to open it. It's not smelly, but it is a bit depressing inside. The opaque window with strange staining is its best feature. It's a squatter, and alarmingly the bum-gun hose is quivering like a vicious snake with the pulsing of changing water pressure.

It's funny how the brain sometimes works to overrule the body. The combination of the snake and the squatter toilet has the effect of instantly locking my bowels. Mission aborted. I wash my hands anyway, and then re-infect them by flipping the latch and pulling the door handle down with my bare hand. I repeat this as nothing happens the first time. Still nothing. I'm now trapped in the toilet of a moving train that will shortly be arriving in Hua Hin with me as a bathroom captive. If this were an aircraft there would be a button you could press to summon help, but no such technology is present here today. After a few more failed attempts to escape I abandon my dignity and bang on the door hoping to attract the attention of anyone passing by. I consider what I would do if

I were outside the door of a toilet with someone banging from inside. It's a multiple-choice answer. A: Try and open the door and provide assistance. B: Go and find the guard and explain there is someone stuck in the toilet. C: slink past and go back to my seat. Today it would seem that most passengers have chosen option C.

I give up banging, and take a pause to think. I would have sat down to do this, but this is a squatter. I figure that I have somewhere between 10 and 20 minutes to get out before my stop. I don't know this for sure, though, as my phone and all my belongings are at my unoccupied seat. Taking stock of a situation always helps, and I take a moment to figure out what might be stopping the door from opening. The latch is open, it's not locked, but when I put my shoulder against the door it just won't move. Focusing on the handle, counter-intuitively I move it to the closed position and, pressing with my shoulder again on the grubby yellowed Formica, I'm suddenly free and back out in the corridor, almost falling over. I dust myself down like I have just been involved in a minor scuffle at the pub and look up and down the carriage and its vestibule. Nothing to see here. No one seems to have noticed my plight, so I'm just going to pretend this never happened and I stroll nonchalantly back to my seat. Most passengers seem glued to the screens of their phones or are

Bang Sue Junction

just gazing out the window, so I'm spared any embarrassment.

Hua Hin is another beautiful Thai railway station, and many regard it as the most beautiful station in the kingdom. Originally opened in 1910, the current building was built in 1926. At one end of the platform is the royal waiting room, once the Sanam Chandra Palace Railway Pavilion, but relocated to Hua Hin in 1967, and here it is now called the Phra Mongkut Klao Pavilion.

Outside the stationmaster's office is quite the shiniest railway bell that I have ever seen. It's so shiny that you need to wear sunglasses to look directly at it. I know that railway workers often get to choose the route they work on, and the most popular ones are allocated by seniority. Might the same be true of stationmasters? Hua Hin would have to be high up the list. Across the tracks a brand-new station is now being constructed that will accommodate new raised lines. I hear that its features are planned to be sympathetic to the design of the original station, which might become a museum. I live in hope, but can't see how the new station will be able to come anywhere close to the original one.

In the ticket office are several wooden boards with a hand-painted timetable. Pieces of paper are taped all over the original version as train schedules change. There is a monitor with live times above the ticket office counter, but the analogue timetable allows you to compare train options throughout the day, depending on how far you're going and how fast you want to get there. A passing monk points at the board I'm studying and asks me where I'm going. There is probably a really good spiritual answer to where I'm going in my life, but I can't think of it quickly enough, so I just tell him I'm going to Bangkok next week. This seems to satisfy his curiosity, and he leaves me alone to study the railway mandala.

The station is on a busy road junction which I would call a roundabout, but actually it's a triangular one-way street. In the middle of the triangleabout sits Locomotive Number 305, built in the United States in 1925. Another one to cross off in my little book.

I can't immediately find transport to my accommodation, but when I practise the procedure of looking like I don't need a lift, a minivan immediately draws up beside me. I think about how in the 1920s I might be in exactly the same spot but a horse-driven carriage would take me down to the Railway Hotel on the beachfront in time for a pre-dinner gin and tonic.

Hua Hin was Thailand's first beach resort, and once the railway line was built it became popular with Bangkok residents looking to escape from the city. I'm staying here for a few days as a bit of R&R, as well as to see its famous railway hotel. In the evening I nurse a cold beer outside a local bar, where I meet Charles, a charming self-made Ugandan millionaire who looks like Omar Sharif would if he were heading off to play a round of golf. Philip Spittle, who I'd met in Chiang Mai, is also in town and later on we feast on good cheese and discuss travel plans.

Before the railway was built this town had been a fishing village, and a fleet of little boats still head out to the shallows of the bay each night to catch squid. '*Hua hin*' means 'stone head', and this is where the fishermen encourage their catch to come up to the surface, using green lamps suspended on booms above their nets. At lunchtime I sit on a rickety boardwalk restaurant and watch them repair their boats. I breathe in the intoxicating fragrance of dried seaweed, fibreglass resin and squid entrails. The freshly caught squid here tastes great, especially with some crispy fried garlic and a really cold beer.

However, I can't linger too long over my lunch today as I have a mission back at the station. Richard Barrow is on the 171 Rapid train that

Cool Hand Matthew

I arrived on, but he is heading down to Su-ngai Kolok and I figure he might need a resupply of rations. I have never attempted to locate a passenger on a train before. I mean one who is not getting off it. In the back of my mind I'm thinking of that scene in *The Man Who Would Be King*; [16] Kipling finds Dravot in a first-class compartment on board the Bombay Mail at Marwar Junction, passing on the message from Brother Carnehan, 'Peachey has gone south for the week'. Richard might just be away for the weekend, but he is definitely headed south too. I'm late, and as I arrive at the railway station the train is already on final approach. I don't have any time to consider what to buy, so I randomly select some cold drinks from a lady in the little platform shop, guessing it's going to be hot on board. I've got to guess which carriage Richard will be in and look in through the windows to find him, but before I start the rendezvous is made easy, as he hops off for a selfie and a quick chat before the guard signals the departure of the train. My work here is done.

Outside the station a policeman pulls up next to me on his scooter. I consider what I might have done wrong. Jaywalking again? Wearing my mask incorrectly? Not wearing any underpants? But he is

---

[16] a story by Rudyard Kipling about two British adventurers in British India, later made into a film

far too focused on balancing his coffee in one hand to notice any legal infringements on my part. This doesn't end well; I have to stop myself from giggling when he tries to get off the bike whilst not spilling his drink, but topples over. The coffee now covers the front of his freshly pressed uniform. You have to feel for him.

The sun sets quickly in this part of the world. One minute it's daytime, and a few moments later the last streaks of sun just over the horizon give way to twilight which is quickly followed by the darkness of the night. Birds tweet, bugs buzz and hungry mosquitoes emerge from their hiding places seeking human flesh and blood until the evening storm arrives. The rains are heavy in these parts, and the drains are quickly overwhelmed by the ankle-deep daily deluge. Bar owners sweep flood water away in the direction of their competitors, but it's nature that's winning this contest. That is with the exception of the local 7/11 store, which has built a wall of sandbags that you have to climb over to get to the door. When the rains arrive this evening I'm inside a small bar down a side street in the middle of town. A lady called Cindy keeps a close eye on my beer in case it needs refreshing. She expertly remembers my beverage preferences, my favourite seat and even my somewhat eclectic musical tastes. The rain continues to pour down outside, cascading off the roof of the bar; it's as though I'm hiding underneath a waterfall.

The places along this road don't serve food, but later on each evening a woman arrives on a rather ingenious bicycle-powered restaurant with various dishes still being cooked as she pedals along the alley. In deference to the weather tonight she is clad in a plastic poncho and has erected a canopy over the top of her kitchen. Fairy lights dangle from the roof, and it all looks very Blade Runner. She calls over to me, and I paddle out to see what's on the menu. It smells great, but I'm unsure what most of it is. Someone once told me that asking what things are defeats the fun of street food, so my approach is to confidently point at a couple of things that might be good. A set of ritual signals, ending with me rubbing my belly and her giving me the thumbs-up. The order is in her field kitchen. I've got some fried rice and on the side some of those pastries that have the appearance of miniature Cornish pasties. But if the average Cornish person tried one of these their head might explode, as they are packed with weapons-grade chilli.

At the back of the bar a couple of drunk young European men play pool and turn the volume of the sound system up when their favourite holiday tunes are played. The bar has invested quite heavily

Bang Sue Junction

in DJ equipment, and the whole bar shakes. Cindy then turns it back down and the process is repeated until one of them heads to the bar. Whilst he is waiting to be served he eyes up the bell above him and decides to hammer it a few times. Customers clap and cheer, and he cheers back, happy to be in the spotlight but not realising why. He does not yet know that he has just committed to buying everyone a drink. I doubt it would stand up in a court of law, but his reputation is now on the line. It's funny to think of the crossover of the use of bells between the railway and the bar industry. If it were reversed there would be a lot of beer on Thai trains, and bars would open and close with the ding of a bell, like last orders used to be announced in the pubs of England.

The billing system usually works in the same way in most Thai bars. There is a little pot on the table, and each time you order a drink, a paper bill is updated at the bar and added back into your pot. I've learned to check this tab regularly, as it's not uncommon for phantom drinks to creep onto the bill, possibly accidentally, or possibly as lucrative additional income for the staff. It's quickly corrected if you spot it, a test of your sobriety and attention to detail. But all is good with my bill tonight and as I fish some damp banknotes out of my pocket I'm surprised to see the way my name is written at the top of my final bill. It says 'Cool

Matthew'. As I've never been one of the cool kids, I point this out to Cindy and ask here why my status has been upgraded. She explains to me that I'm known as Cool Matthew because I always ask for a fan, which they place next to my table to provide a breeze to cut through the humidity. It would seem that I am one of the cool kids here after all.

The following morning I take a walk along the beach to the Railway Hotel, which is now known as the Centara Grand Beach Resort. The hotel would not exist were it not for the construction of the Southern Line, and Hua Hin might still be a little fishing village were it not for the arrival of both. When the hotel first opened its doors in 1922 it would have been the place to stay in these parts, and it still is to this very day. Designed by an Italian architect, Alfredo Rigazzi, the style of the property is distinctly European. It proved to be a draw to both the well-off in Bangkok as well as those passing through en route to Singapore.

I'm shown around by General Manager Jan, who opens up some hidden treasures, including the Railway Suite, one of the best rooms in the hotel, carefully preserved to reflect the history of the hotel. The connection to the Southern Line lives on, and I'm delighted to discover a room full of hotel memorabilia dating back to the early days. As we wander through the gardens I sense a familiarity with the white-painted wooden verandas encircling the guest rooms. This hotel was a location for the 1984 film *The Killing Fields*, reimagined as the Cambodian Hotel Le Phnom. David Puttnam and the crew stayed at the hotel whilst they were filming, and Jan shows me a group photograph of them posing where we have been standing. Inside the hotel, one restaurant is themed loosely in the style of a railway station, complete with clocks and signs. It's a bullseye for how to do heritage rail tourism.

The rains come and go. The best forecasting tool that I have discovered is the pool bar at the place I'm staying. The staff spot the storms approaching from some way off along the coast, and the bar captain judges the very last moment to batten down the hatches, setting off the staff to race around, packing absolutely everything up before it's too late. Anyone without an umbrella is going to get a free torrential shower. I like to play chicken here and be the last person out before the rain hits us.

As my time draws to a close in Hua Hin I need to arrange a train back to Bangkok. The trains coming up from the south are still heavily delayed, sometimes by as much as a day. When I visit the railway station to buy a ticket the man behind the counter thinks I'm a bit crazy as there is no way of knowing what time the train might arrive. But I tell him that I have a cunning plan. As I have found on most of the lines in Thailand, there are usually at least two sleeper services a couple of hours apart passing through in the early morning. So my thinking is that if I aim for a later one and it's delayed, I might catch an earlier train further up the line, which logically might be delayed by about the same amount of time.

When I wake the next morning, the sky is grey and the sea flat calm. I hate early starts. As I have predicted, my train, Number 38, is several hours behind schedule, but I have time to catch the faster overnight sleeper on its way up the line from Hat Yai. Most of the taxi drivers are sensibly still asleep, so I have to wake one up. Taxis in Hua Hin are a strange minivan conversion with an enclosed cab but open back, making them look like Tonka toys.

Back at the station my plan works perfectly. My original ticket is refunded, and a new one for the approaching 32 Special Express is issued. It's 500 baht more expensive, as second class is in a sleeper carriage rather than just a seated day train. I'm actually 2 baht short, but he lets me off. It's funny that I'm normally the sort of person who wants to be early, the first on the platform, at the front of the queue. I find the possibility of being late and missing a train highly stressful. But today I'm in an unusually relaxed state. Then something that has never happened before on this trip. The man at the ticket counter tells me, 'Go, go now!' I don't think that this is because he is bored of talking to me, but rather because he is worried that I might miss my train.

The black sky has commenced dropping its ordnance on the earth, and rain is now splashing with its impact onto the concrete platform. From the shelter of the covered part of the station I look southwards in anticipation of spotting the approaching locomotive. Then the thought crosses my mind that this is going to be a long train and I have no idea where my carriage will be. My ticket has been printed in Thai, so I ask the stationmaster what he thinks. He suggests that I need to be at the rear of the train, but I'm not going out there in this weather, so I huddle with a small group of passengers under the cover of the roof.

I spot the lights of the train in the distance about the same time as a guard rings the bell and I realise that I'm going to get wet. Very wet. Someone told me once that you get wetter running in the rain than walking in it, something to do with forward velocity and airflow. I have to tell you that it makes no difference at all. After getting soaked in a 30-second walk I start to jog, or at least move as quickly as I can with my bags. I have never experienced the interrogation technique of waterboarding, but I'm sure that running whilst wearing a face mask in an intense downpour must be a similar experience.

There is often that moment with an approaching train when your carriage passes you by in the direction that you have come from – unless you are in somewhere like Japan, where the exact spot to stand is marked for you on the platform. I have to retrace my steps quite a way when Carriage 11 passes me by. By the time I reach it the attendant has opened the door and is sheltering in the vestibule. I know what he's thinking. It's disappointment that I'm about to mess up his spotless recently cleaned floor. I show him my ticket, which actually turns out to be for Berth 11 in Carriage Number 2 – at the other end of the train. I'm pleased that my big bag has wheels, as I have to steer it through six carriages to reach my seat.

It's early enough that most passengers are sensibly still in bed, and the attendant is packing up the berths from those who have left the train at Hua Hin. I'm directed to one that's already been reset in day mode and settle in as best as I can. The carriage is freezing cold and I'm soaked to the skin. I consider stripping off, but instead I mop myself

Bang Sue Junction

down with tissues, then in my day bag find a shemagh that, if I stretch it, covers most of my body in a form of mummification. I don't usually get cold on trains; normally I'm too hot. On my travels in Siberia I'm used to having to cool things down rather than heat them up. I have the secret key and a set of spanners to open windows. I happen to know that if you push the toilet roof panel open on old Chinese carriages, cool air ventilates through the corridor. The only time I have been close to cold on board a train was on an Amtrak sleeper. The trick there is to apply cellophane wrap to the air vents. But none of this knowledge is going to help me today. Fortunately the sun is soon poking through the clouds, and in the style of a lizard on a rock, I bask in the warmth of its radiation.

As I'm writing some notes the head of a man opposite me emerges from behind his blue curtain. He looks about furtively and smiles when he sees me. His dark skin emphasises an enormous set of perfect shiny white teeth stretching from ear to ear. Complete with long hair and goatee beard he's obviously, in a Thai way, very hip. His smile is contagious and I have no choice but to smile back at him before returning to my notes. A few minutes later the curtains are pulled back and whilst trying not to stare, glancing across I find myself looking at a massive ghetto blaster, the kind kids used to breakdance with in the 1980s. Then the music starts. No one else seems to bat an eyelid, and he's captured me with his cheeky grin. I can't possibly suggest it's too loud after the exchange of smiles, so I take it as part of the onboard entertainment and suck in the experience.

By the time the train arrives in the outskirts of Bangkok the storms have passed by and it's a nice afternoon. It's the usual drill past Bang Sue Junction as the rails navigate through small stations and level crossings, crawling into the heart of the city. I wave at the railway people but they stare beyond me and the train. Like people who live under the flight path of an airport but can't hear the noise of the planes, they have achieved a mental state of removing the passing trains from their minds.

Bang Sue Junction

Chapter Fifteen
Heavy Metal

I have arranged to hook up with Richard Barrow again, this time for a new mission, and one that neither of us knows how it might turn out. Those in the know talk in whispers about a train yard behind Thonburi Station. If you manage to reach inside as far as the engine shed, you might discover the SRT's collection of working steam locomotives. It's not officially open to the public, but on the other hand it's not closed either. Like many things in Thailand, this is open to interpretation. We will just have to see how far we can get.

By the time I find the right riverside ferry pier Richard is already there waiting for me. When the next boat approaches I wobble down the metal

Bang Sue Junction

gangplank with some care, as the last thing I fancy today is an unplanned dip in the river. I don't know what's in there, but I do know that I don't want to drink it, or be eaten by it. The technique is to match the resonance of the gangplank's movement by swaying with it. After a carefully choreographed docking manoeuvre using a series of whistle signals, we are underway upriver, the narrow hull of the boat easily cutting through the slight chop. Nothing beats being on the Chao Phraya River – it's a refuge from the traffic and street life. Best of all, a stiff breeze from the forward momentum keeps you cool. I squeeze the boat ticket tightly in my hand in case it gets blown overboard, and Richard keeps up an encyclopaedic commentary about the buildings that line the riverbanks.

Our stop has been named the Railway Pier, now in front of the Siriraj Hospital building, but once the site of the original Bangkok Noi Station. After being bombed by the Allies during the Second World War it was rebuilt before being relocated a few hundred metres up the line to Thonburi in order to make space for the construction of the hospital. In a nod to the past there is an open display space, and at its centre is the freshly painted and polished Japanese steam locomotive, Number 950, coincidentally built in 1950. I make a note of it in my book when Richard isn't looking, just in

Heavy Metal

case he thinks that I have turned into a full-on trainspotter over the last few weeks. But when we stop for a coffee I discover that it's the other way around. He produces a guide to the steam trains of the SRT from his bag and explains that we might need this later on. I take note of the bogies, wheel configurations, age and nationality of the five steam locomotives in case there is a test.

We navigate through the hospital buildings and along the busy road towards Thonburi, eventually meeting the track, which comes much further back towards the river than the station in order to allow shunting trains out of the yard. Following it, we soon spot an old water tower, and then the engine shed itself. In front of us there is a roadside entrance to the yard and a sign confirming that we have found Thonburi Locomotive Garage. The current building was built for the Royal State Railway of Siam in 1947, and as well as looking after the steam engines, its occupants are also now busy repairing the SRT's ageing diesel locomotives.

The entrance gate to the yard is along one side of the tracks nestled alongside to a khlong leading back to the river. There is a fence here festooned with signs. Public urination is banned, as is feeding the dogs. What sort of dogs might they be? Local friendly soi dogs or vicious guard dogs? I can't find a sign saying No Entry or Keep Out, which gives our reason for being here some legitimacy. An exchange of purposeful glances, and we continue inside the fence.

If you have ever been to a place where you probably shouldn't be, you will know the importance of self-confidence. If you can convince yourself that you belong somewhere, you look like you do belong there. Past the gate we come across a group of oil-smeared workers taking a break in the shade of the building. They are playing cards at a low table encircled by camping chairs, and when they spot us they give us a wave and a smile. There is no sign that we are not welcome. We try to look natural, now standing at the open track doors to the repair shed. Forgive me for calling it a shed, as engine sheds are enshrined in British railways. If you prefer the official title, please think of this as a locomotive garage.

A security guard keeps an eye on us from a distance, but stays inside his hut. So far, so good. We have now successfully completed the first stage of our plan. Our next move is to enter the shed itself, which we do after pausing outside for a few minutes to normalise our presence. Then we walk inside with purpose, as though we might be here on some form of official inspection. There are no shouts from anyone, and no attack dogs chase after us. My eyes don't have much time to adjust to the shadows of the shed before we encounter our first problem. An old General Electric diesel locomotive nearby has started growling and a plume of dark smoke has erupted from its roof. The engine is moving towards us. For the record, it's a UM12C built in the 1960s and refurbished here, but I don't have time to note its number. With a sense of urgency, we cross the rails inside the shed to be clear of its path. High above us the driver sounds his horn a couple of times, stops, then when he is confident we are out of the way, he resumes along the track to a repair station deep inside.

My brain is still processing the health and safety implications of what has just happened when another hazard materialises. This time it's a small crane carrying a huge lump of engine which dangles and sways in front like a wrecking ball. I assume that the driver knows what he is doing, but as he gets closer and closer I begin to wonder ... what if he doesn't? There isn't much room to manoeuvre in here. It all happens very fast, but I'm mesmerised and witness it in slow motion. The metal plates on the ground between the tracks are slippery with grease and gunk, and care is needed to stay upright. I manage to step away to one side but don't judge it very well, and I watch the engine swing like a pendulum towards me. Richard grabs me at the last moment and pulls

Bang Sue Junction

me further back as the crane wobbles past. We both know what the other is thinking. A dead foreigner inside the engine shed would not be a good railway PR story. I say to myself, for goodness' sake, make a better effort to stay alive, Matthew. I'm not sure if I say it out loud or not.

By this point we are far enough inside the shed that we have passed the working tracks and immediate dangers of the engineering works. In front of us now are just dusty trains and piles of assorted parts that look like mostly junk. I call it junk, but if you put it up for auction it would probably be worth a fortune as historic railwayana. The locomotives in front of us are not any old trains, but the historic collection of Thai steam locomotives. We have found the Thai trainspotting holy grail.

The five working locomotives are pushed together on two lines at the far side of the shed. They were all built in Japan. The oldest are a pair of C56 class engines that are the last remaining of forty-six imported during the Second World War. Originally used to transport troops, amazingly Nos 713 and 715 were still in passenger service for short runs until 1982. Other than the train numbers, if you are a real trainfan you will recognise their classic 2-6-0 wheel configuration. Behind them are a pair of Pacific locomotives, 824 and 850, dating from 1949 and 1950. They have a distinctive 4-6-2 set of wheels. Finally, at the back is a single Mikado locomotive, Number 953, one of seventy imported around 1950, also in full service until 1982.

If only steam engines could talk. Just think of the tales they could tell, especially the wartime C56s. It's wonderful that they have been so well looked after, and I'm really sad that on this trip I'm not going to travel on one. In just a few weeks' time the Pacific locomotives will be used as a pair to haul a tourist train on a run up to Ayutthaya: a day trip by steam for the princely sum of 299 baht. The fact that these locos are still run by the SRT and used for train tourism is wonderful.

Now a little more relaxed about our surroundings, we continue to work around the steam locomotives towards the back of the shed, where we find a couple of diesel engines in middle of the train equivalent of a heart transplant, their innards removed and laid out on the ground awaiting surgery. When we are satisfied that we have seen all that it is possible to see, we work our way back to the way we came in, taking care not to trip over in the oily shadows between the rows of diesel engines. Sunlight streams in through the open doors of the shed, and outside them I can now see another train. It's a distinctively orange-fronted Alstom AD24C, probably built in

Bang Sue Junction

the mid-1970s. The snag this time is that as there are trains on tracks on either side of us we have nowhere to seek refuge. The train driver is revving the engine slightly menacingly. He sounds the twin horns mounted on the roof and begins to advance towards us. It's loud inside the shed, and I have to shout to Richard, 'I think it's coming in right here?' – the inference in my voice that we might be in a sticky situation. Talk about stating the obvious. We stare at the approaching engine is case it's an apparition rather than 70 tonnes of metal headed our way. But in a way it is an apparition, as the train's destination is an optical illusion. It's actually on another line, one that skirts around the shed and onwards to the railway station. This being the third near miss in an hour, we call it a day, and have a cold drink and some railway rice on the platform at Thonburi. What a day! – rail enthusiasm on a whole new level.

I can't seem to relax on my last few days in Bangkok. There was a time when reading a book by the pool used to make me feel good, but this indulgence has clearly worn off. I just want to be on the rails with an open window and a breeze in my face. Bells, food vendors, chatter and a constantly changing view are all I'm after. It's the new me. So, on my last day in Thailand I decide to head back over to Hua Lamphong for one final time and catch a train to Bang Sue Junction.

Heavy Metal

I nod at the temperature-check man as I enter the station and join a short queue at the ticket counter. It costs just 2 baht to get to Bang Sue on an Ordinary train, which has to be one of the best railway deals on the planet. Train 233 is waiting for me on Platform 5. The carriage is one of the oldest I have ever seen. It has bare wooden seats, tarnished steel window shutters and a dull ochre paint on the walls inside. A series of little fans line the ceiling, each one controlled by an individual switch beside the window. We slowly clatter along the now familiar route out of the city and it takes about 20 minutes to reach Bang Sue Junction. I realise that I have no idea where this train is going to. Perhaps I should have remained on board – a mystery train tour would have been fun. But I step down onto the middle platform and watch it head off down the line, destination unknown. The station is busy, not just with passengers but with office workers eating lunch, and I decide to join them for one final train-based feast.

I find Chompoo towards the end of the line of platform vendors, and order the railway rice and a lime and soda served so cold that at first it sticks to the plastic tablecloth. Sitting here on my chopped log seat in the shade of the main platform I'm in the perfect spot to contemplate life on the rails in Thailand.

Bang Sue Junction

I'm thinking about all the things that I have seen over the past few weeks, and also about what lies ahead. Thailand is committed to a high-speed rail future, which will include modern stations, hermetically sealed carriages and modern diesel-electric locomotives. I feel guilty that this is not the railway that I would prefer, but you can't hold this progress back. I have proved to myself this trip that I'm just as happy in a third-class carriage with an open window as in a brand-new Chinese sleeper with wifi, television and a hot shower. Ordinary trains and the current express sleepers between them are a perfect combination to cover the ground in a country this size. I only hope that the two railway worlds will exist side by side in future, at least for some years to come. But then I think about the bigger picture once again. The rail route across South East Asia from Beijing to Singapore via Laos, Thailand and Malaysia. The South East Asian Express. That's going to be quite a trip, and something to really look forward to.

I order another lime soda, and Chompoo asks me where I'm going. 'I'm going back to England tonight,' I tell her with a slight lump in my throat, 'but I'm coming back soon.' My emotion surprises even me. She smiles and says 'You like watching trains?' *'Mak mak,'* I tell her – 'so much' – and I explain that I like travelling on them even more than I do looking at them. 'You come see me

Heavy Metal

again,' she says. I promise her that I will. Just at that very moment, with hopefully prophetic timing, the stationmaster rings the bell. My wishes have been blessed. I just hope that Bang Sue Junction will still be here when I return.

Bang Sue Junction

Afterword

The first long-distance passenger train to depart from Krun Thep Aphiwat Central Terminal was the Rapid 171 headed for Su-ngai Kolok. It was pulled out of the station by a new Chinese Qishuyan CDA5B1 Ultraman locomotive on 19 January 2023. The Bang Sue Grand sign is still on the front of the building. The reported cost of a replacement sign is 33 million baht (£742,000).

The Thailand Pass registration system was finally closed in July 2022, and in October 2022 there ceased to be any requirement to show proof of vaccination. The borders with Laos Cambodia have now fully reopened.

Freight Train Number 707 was derailed by a bomb on the line from Hat Yai to the border at

Pandang Besar on 3 December 2022. Three days later a second explosion at the scene of the recovery operation killed three workers and injured several more. The line to Malaysia was closed again, but is now back up and running with daily trains and increased security.

In December 2022 a tourist fell to his death from the Nam Tok train at the Tham Kra Sae bridge. He was reported to be posing for a selfie at the open door of the carriage.

The replacement housing for the Bun Romsai community is due to be finished in 2025, but the bulldozers have already moved in on their trackside homes.

Bangkok Station has now been officially renamed Hua Lamphong. It is still running over sixty local and tourist trains a day, including all the services on the Eastern Line. If you walk onto the platforms you will now find steam locomotives on permanent display. Plans are in place to preserve the station and build upon its heritage. Thailand has woken up to the possibilities of railway tourism.

Bang Sue Junction is still operating as a stop for local passenger trains until the new elevated line

Afterword

from Krun Thep Aphiwat Central Terminal to Hua Lamphong is completed in the years to come.

I'm still seeing an osteopath to fix my shoulder. He suspects that I have had a dislocated rib. It was either the massage or the bike crash.

I named my elephants Boon Nam (good fortune) and Kob Sook (heart full of happiness). I'm going to take a picture of them in my home and take it back to show Aoi in Chiang Mai

Bang Sue Junction

Glossary

Bangkok Noi – once Bangkok's riverside station, now relocated to nearby Thonburi.

Bangkok Railway Station – also known (incorrectly until 2023) as Hua Lamphong, the site of the original station nearby.

Bang Sue Grand – the interim name for Krung Thep Aphiwat Central Terminal.

BTS – Bangkok Transit System, elevated mass transport system, known to many as the Skytrain.

Cambodian Express – nickname for the third-class train that travels twice each day from Bangkok to the Cambodian border at Aranyaprathet. I understand that in the next few years it will become a real night train, reaching as far as Phnom Penh.

Insurgency Express – unfortunate nickname for the trains heading through the southern provinces to the border at Su-ngai Kolok.

International Express – semi-official name for the sleeper train that used to run from Bangkok to Butterworth (in Malaysia, the jumping-off point for Penang). The train now finishes at the Padang Besar frontier with Malaysia.

Krungthep MRT Station – now renamed Bangkok (Hua Lamphong) MRT.

Krung Thep Aphiwat Central Terminal – King Vajiralongkorn bestowed this name on the new Bangkok Station. It translates as 'Bangkok's prosperity'.

MRT – Metropolitan Rapid Transport (also Mass Rapid Transport) running above and below ground in and around Bangkok.

Ordinary train – third-class slow train that usually stops at every station.

Paknam Railway – Thailand's first railway, a narrow-gauge private line running the 13 miles

Glossary

(21 km) from Hua Lamphong to Paknam. It opened in 1893 and closed in 1959.

Rapid train – multiple unit with air conditioning. Faster than an Ordinary train.

Special Express – modern long-distance train, usually offering seats and sleeper carriages.

Thonburi – the relocated Bangkok Noi Station.

Ultraman – nickname for new generation of Chinese CRRC Qishuyan CDA5B1 locomotives coming into service.

Wongwian Yai – Bangkok's third original railway station, the terminus of the Mae Klong Line.

Acknowledgements

I would like to thank everyone who encouraged me to write this book and also those who helped make it happen.

To Keith Parsons, without whom I would not yet have written a single word.

To my editor, Caroline Petherick, for once again fixing my bad writing habits.

To Mark Hudson, Colin Brooks and Josh Gibson for their work on the design of this book. Thanks for creating just the right 'feel'.

To Richard Barrow for helping me understand the inner workings of Thai trains. Let's bring hard hats and high-vis vests next time.

To Tim Russell for book photography and for introducing me to the underbelly of life next to the rails. Viva Jack's Bar!

To Dr Siriphong Preutthipan, President of the Thai Railway Foundation, for help with the history and behind-the-scenes tours.

To David McNeil at the Royal Geographical Society, London, for help with the Collections.

Acknowledgements

To Ben Svasti Thomson, British Honorary Consul Chiang Mai, and the officers of Wing 41, Royal Thai Airforce.

To Nick, Mathieu and Malika at Ball Watch Company. The sleeper train compartments on this adventure were bathed in the soft glow of tritium light.

To Sarah Murray for reminding me that railway stations are as important to me as the trains that inhabit them.

To Kiwi and her mother, Mango, for keeping me alive at the Mae Klong Market. Always keep three sleepers back.

To Aki for his travel advice and his smiles, despite his being shot and gassed in the Iran–Iraq war.

To Aoi and all who work at the Elephant Parade social enterprise. You are amazing.

To my early reader group, Philip Spittle, Rob Woodcock, Neil Walker and Chris Ring for such helpful feedback.

To Jan Weishet for helping me reimagine life on the rails in Siam from the original Railway Hotel in Hua Hin, now the Centara Grand Beach Resort.

To the staff and wonderful crowd at Jack's Bar, the centre of my social universe in Bangkok.

To all the proud, efficient and polite employees of the SRT who looked after me as I travelled throughout the land of smiles.

About the Author

Matthew Woodward is a rail-based adventurer and writer based in Chichester, West Sussex. Previously living and working in Edinburgh, he decided to quit the rat race after a successful career in drinks marketing. He now writes for a variety of publications on long range rail travel. He is a Fellow of the Royal Geographical Society. A self-confessed coffee addict, he carries an espresso machine wherever he travels. *Bang Sue Junction* is his fifth book.

For more information please visit:

www.matthew-woodward.com

Bang Sue Junction

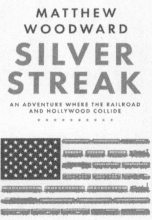

Bang Sue Junction

If you enjoyed *Bang Sue Junction*, then you might like to also read *The Railway to Heaven*

The Railway to Heaven

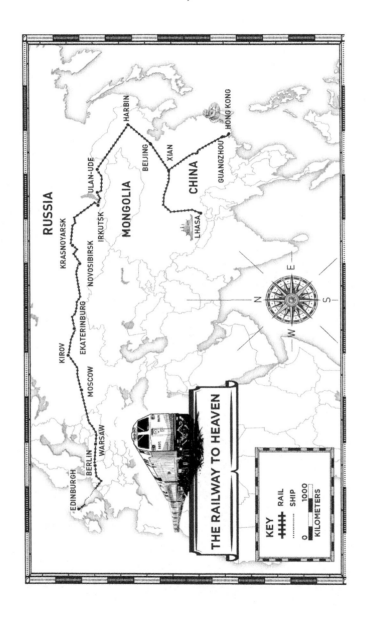

246

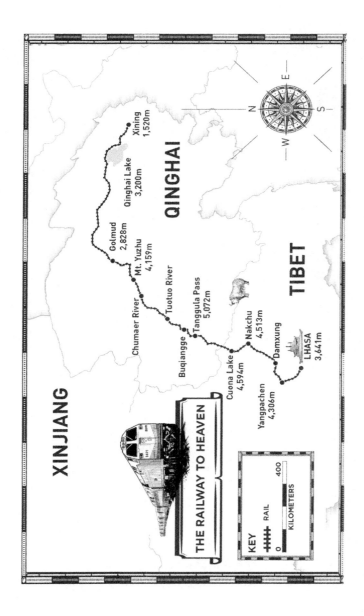

The Railway to Heaven

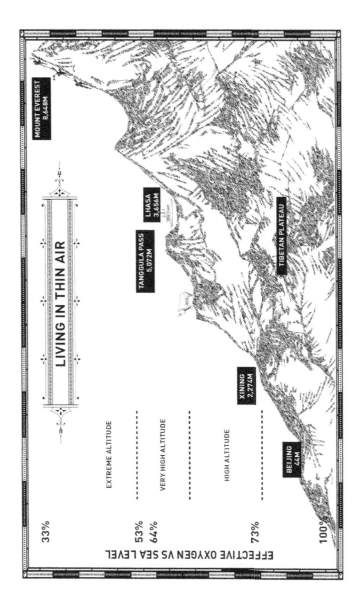

Chapter One
The Man Who Would Be King

Tenzing strides ahead of me up the steep cobbled path towards the monastery. Looking upwards at him getting progressively further ahead, I feel frustrated not to be able to match his pace; my body is used to getting far more oxygen than is available in the thin air up here. I have to squint as I look upwards at him. The cloudless and saturated blue sky behind him is strangely ethereal. Despite the cold, the rising sun warms us, reflecting off the whitewashed buildings.

In many parts of the world I get introduced to people calling themselves Johnny (or its local equivalent), who obviously have a real name but choose to keep it secret. I

The Railway to Heaven

guess they have found it's too hard for foreigners to pronounce or remember. But Tenzing really is called Tenzing, a popular name not just in Nepal but also here on the Tibetan Plateau. There is something about him that I put down to a military bearing and appearance, but I haven't asked him about his background. I suspect he has a particular set of skills that I hope won't be needed during our time together. Nonethless it's reassuring to know that he's probably trained and prepared for any eventuality. Relaxed but confident, Tenzing is in many ways the perfect travel companion. His best asset is his smile. He smiles brightly when he speaks to anyone, and seems to have friends absolutely everywhere. He is proof that positive body language and politeness can get you just about anything you want.

Every few minutes he turns back to me and asks if I want to stop for a break, but I'm stubborn and determined to keep going. Unacclimatised to the altitude as I am, this small hill is proving a significant challenge to my feeble legs and lungs. Pilgrims and kids stride effortlessly past me, spinning huge brass prayer wheels as we make our way towards the entrance to the main courtyard. Spotting a bench on a rocky outcrop I have to stop – not only due to the urgent demands of my body, but also because I need time for my senses to take in the emerging scene in front of me. Suntanned monks in their dark haematite-coloured robes are directing visitors as they enter the monastery. Pilgrims wave their arms in a mad fashion and whirl about at the bottom of the big stone steps. Some even

The Man Who Would Be King

crawl forwards on their bellies. Hypnotic sounds of bells ringing and Tibetan horns. Clouds of incense mixed with the scent of local flowers and juniper berries. Pinch myself hard. Have I arrived onto the film set of one of my favourite Kipling films, 'The Man Who Would be King'?

Once inside the outer walls, we walk together up the main path, where a long line of people, mainlywomen and children, are waiting. Many of the younger kids are crying and screaming, while the older ones just look miserable. This is very unusual in Tibet. Tenzing puts his smile on and leans over a little fence to speak to a monk at the entrance to the nondescript stone building. Not sure what to do, I stand at a respectable distance behind the line. Without explanation Tenzing returns and gestures for me to follow him through the crowd, whereupon another monk appears and opens a small side door that I hadn't noticed until then. The door is quickly shut behind us before the crowd notice us, leaving us alone and in the dark. As my eyes adjust, Tenzing explains that the monks here hold blessings for ill children in the afternoons. Our arrival has coincided with the Tibetan equivalent of a long wait at accident and emergency.

But we are not here for a blessing, and I don't yet know the purpose of our visit. I have a suspicion that we're now inside a building that we probably shouldn't be in. Around us lie dusty wooden cabinets and cupboards on a rough stone floor. Trickles of light penetrate through the cracks

The Railway to Heaven

between the wooden planks of the heavy shutters covering the windows, and once Tenzing has found the switch, a solitary light bulb glows dimly above us.

I'm about to step forwards, but there is something unusual about the floor. Tenzing's arm holds me back and steadies me. I begin to make out strange shapes. In front of me on the ground is a complex painting made of many coloured sands: a mandala. It's about 3 metres square with incredible detail. The purpose of our visit here is for my introductory lesson from Tenzing in the symbolism of Tibetan Buddhism, and he explains to me how meditative monks have constructed this intricate design to represent the transient nature of material life. You have to concentrate hard and somehow imagine the shapes of the mandala inside yourself. The circles become a never-ending life, and proof that everything is connected. I stare at the pattern until I'm a bit cross-eyed and dizzy. Unused to the practice of meditation, I fail to reach enlightenment today. I shall have to return to complete my spiritual journey another time. With my first lesson over, I'm free to examine the objects in the cabinets nearby, while Tenzing goes into a passageway to look for the way through into the next room. It's strangely peaceful to be almost alone in here whilst still being able to hear the commotion outside.

When Tenzing returns he looks slightly concerned. This wouldn't mean anything to you unless you knew that normally his facial expression is one of beaming happiness, so even looking normal is a sign that something might be wrong. The trouble is that the doors in front of us and behind us are both locked shut. I have no fear, though. After all, I'm with a man who I suspect has been trained to break out of places more secure than this. He scans the room, tries a few other doors, and then jumps up to see if he can get to a little window. They are all securely locked. He pushes and adjusts the position of a couple of the cabinets, looking for a hidden doorway. I can't help but smile despite our circumstances. I'm back in one of my favourite childhood movies...all I need is a bull whip and the right hat. But dark thoughts cross my oxygen-starved mind. I hope Tenzing has a plan, otherwise a hundred years from now a monk might open the door and discover a couple of skeletons next to the mandala. Tenzing starts to bang on the little door, and I join in, as much for moral support as for the extra noise. But with the cacophony outside, no one can hear us.

The Railway to Heaven

Chapter Two
The Edinburgh Explorers Club

South Learmont Gardens is a quiet Edinburgh crescent with attractive Georgian architecture. There is nothing particularly Scottish about it: you could mistake the road and its buildings for the centre of another city of the period, like Bath or Bristol. Idling along the wide pavement I pass elegant town houses, now mainly converted into expensive flats, embassies and boutique hotels. Above the front steps of number 13 is a red awning, and a well-manicured planter sits either side of the front door. A little brass plaque next to the bell push says 'Channings Hotel'. Climbing the stairs and walking past the reception area, I turn left into one of the front rooms. It was the sort of room that the management of the hotel didn't expect you to linger in, but even so they had furnished it with a pair of big chairs and a

The Railway to Heaven

table with a chessboard. At one time it would have been the parlour of the house next door, but at Channings it was just a room to pass through on the way to the restaurant or your bedroom. My adventure mentor, Keith Parsons, was already there and was busy making notes, his reading glasses perched on the end of his nose. He has drawn a complex looking flowchart, but as I can't read upside down I don't yet know what his new big idea might be. On the table sits the ceremonial and rather battered biscuit tin in which we store the maps and plans of the Edinburgh Explorers Club. Anyone can join our club, but as we haven't told anyone else about it there are currently just two members. Tea arrives in due course and we chat over possible plans, every now and then disturbed by guests looking for directions to the lift. They probably wondered, unaware of the history of the room, why we were sitting here. But we knew. The original house we were in had been the home of Sir Ernest Henry Shackleton between 1904 and 1907. Surely there couldn't be a more inspirational place to plan my adventures than the very parlour room where Sir Ernest would have sat, reading the papers and making arrangements for his next polar expedition.

History suggests, however, that Shackleton's time in Scotland was not the greatest period of his life. Having been rejected as a full-time officer by the Royal Navy, failing to win a seat as member of parliament in the 1906 general election, and also investing in a doomed business venture involving the transport of Russian troops from the

The Edinburgh Explorers Club

Far East, he bounced back, taking on a job as president of the Scottish Geographical Society. He lived in Edinburgh until he set off on the Nimrod Expedition to find the magnetic south pole. Having met his grand-daughter at the Royal Geographical Society in London, Keith and I were bitten by the Shackleton bug, and spent much time reading and researching his expeditions. Our hobby took us to shipyards, graveyards and buildings across the country. Although Shackleton was very much a public figure in his own lifetime, he was almost forgotten during much of the 20th century and it is only in more recent times that he has begun to be admired as the inspirational leader most regard him as today.

The meeting of the Edinburgh Explorers Club today was a short one, as I had agreed to give a talk to a few people about my travels in Siberia. Tea and biscuits consumed, Keith and I headed to a little meeting room across the hall. We liked this room as it actually contained a few Shackleton artefacts: letters, a bottle of scotch, and early photographs, almost hidden in a glass-fronted cabinet behind the door. My presentation was a bit rushed, and the projector bulb was so dark that I had to describe some of my pictures, but the audience seemed to find my new career as a long-range rail adventurer interesting enough to ask lots of questions. I don't have a lot in common with Sir Ernest, except that he too had to fund his exploration with lecture tours, and we have both travelled to places that were extremely cold. But he got to talk about cute penguins and ships, and I get to talk about rabid dogs and trains.

After the talk we all moved into the bar, where further questions came thick and fast. And then the question that always gets asked: 'Where to next?' The answer was slightly complicated, so I unfolded a map and spread it out on the bar top. It had various routes marked in different inks, and annotations scribbled all along the lines that extended from Europe to Asia. I pointed out the various borders, no-go zones and visa complications of each of the coloured lines. Everyone loves an aspiring adventurer with a map; it somehow gives your plans more respectability. The answer was yet to be decided. After a few pints of Deuchars my audience thinned out, so Keith and I made plans for a late-night curry with Mark Hudson, another close supporter of my adventures. I don't know how many poppadums are the correct adult human portion, but that night we consumed several large piles of them whilst I explained my options in more detail, waiting for some reaction. Mark, normally the 'that doesn't sound very safe' kind of person, is at times touchingly concerned for my personal wellbeing. On the other hand, Keith is the 'what are you waiting for' friend, more interested in bigger and badder adventures, even ones that feel out of my reach. Together they make a well-balanced double act of different schools of thought. I am inspired by the energy of others, and I also use moments like this to make myself commit to doing things that are outside my comfort zone. Once I've said I'm going to do it, there's no going back – it's a binding contract with myself. So that evening, by the time the chicken madras arrived I felt I was ready to commit to a plan, but there seemed to be two competing routes: one was to take the train from Beijing to Lhasa, only possible since 2006, and the other to explore the less well known Trans-Manchurian route through Siberia, the long way round: by-passing Mongolia, going directly into China's north-eastern region, Manchuria, and then down to Beijing. High on the endorphin rush of weapons-grade curry, I realised that there was nothing to stop me combining the two. To travel on the longest and then the highest railways in the world together, as one grand adventure. I would take the train from Edinburgh to Lhasa.

Back then, in that beer-and-chilli-fuelled moment, it all seemed very simple.

The Railway to Heaven

Chapter Three
The Manchurian Candidate

Back at my desk the next day I made some calls to people I knew and trusted, to check the feasibility of the idea. I wanted to know if it could become a real plan. My notes were hand written on cards laid out in order of priority, top to bottom, left to right. When I'd worked in a large company, over time I had learnt the value of a well-organised desk. I used to have one until facilities management introduced the concept of hot desking, and then I lost my personal space and, along with it, its good order. Desks became transitory and unloved spaces where only boring things happened. Nothing interesting could be found on them, just the rubbish of the previous user.

But now, determined to have a place of inspiration in my new life as a rail adventurer, I had created a desk space to

The Railway to Heaven

help me deliver my plans. Only pens of the same type were allowed in the same pot; notebooks were colour coded; and I wrote in each book in different coloured inks to remind me where I was. Next to my banker's lamp was a small collection of artefacts and icons to help inspire me. These included a piece of wood from the hull of Sir Francis Chichester's round-the-world yacht Gypsy Moth V, a late uncle's WW2 commando dagger, an ornate metal and glass Russian Railways teacup, and a framed cartoon I had been given that depicted someone who looked rather like me (with an unusually large head) arriving at the fireside cooking spot of a tribe of happy cannibals. The caption underneath read 'Unwittingly, Matthew stepped out of the jungle and into headhunter folklore forever'. It always made me smile. My desk was the place where I needed to turn those curry-fuelled ideas into reality.

Confirmation that the journey was actually going to be possible came a day or two later when the company that fixes my visas had spoken to their contact in Beijing. I had become quite used to the red tape of getting visas and tickets for long train journeys, but this new adventure was at times an exercise in lateral thought. To visit Tibet you needed a special permit, which would only be issued if you had an approved guide from the government and approved accommodation. There were several grades of permit, ranging from travel just on the Tibetan Plateau through to one for climbing Mount Everest. But there was a snag. You couldn't get this permit without a visa first, but if you applied for a tourist visa for

The Manchurian Candidate

China and said you were going to travel to Tibet it would apparently be refused. This was a Catch 22.

The work-around recommendation was a strange one, but it seemed to be the only solution: apply for a Chinese visa with simpler travel plans and then, once it had been issued, change the plans and apply for the Tibet permit. But the application needed to include confirmed hotel bookings, and a detailed travel itinerary, so I worked on a touristic trip around the sights of China and made some reservations. The application went off to the embassy in London – but I couldn't wait for the outcome of this process, as I needed to ensure I was able to get a reservation made on other trains, most importantly the Trans-Manchurian that would take me from Moscow to Beijing the long way around. Instead of crossing Mongolia and the Gobi Desert as in my first Trans-Siberian adventure, I would head further eastwards in Siberia, and then south into Manchuria, to Harbin, and down through the rustbelt of the provinces of north-eastern China. If I was refused a Tibet permit I would need a Plan B once I reached Beijing. For the time being I put Plan B to the back of my mind.

In between long bouts of form filling I read quite a lot, trying to get a feel for the places that I would be visiting. Books about conflict in Manchuria, books about tackling the Himalayas from the Chinese side, and climbing books about the potentially fatal problems at high altitude. They were a luxury that I didn't have room

The Railway to Heaven

to carry, so I photocopied vital pages and made copious notes in the style of school exam revision. Not only were the books too big and heavy, but they would probably also get me in trouble if spotted by customs officials. My understanding was that any book that shows Tibet as a country on a map is prohibited in China, along with any pictures of the current (14th) Dalai Lama.

Emails started to arrive from my visa agents in London and Moscow, most of them encouraging. I updated the cards on my desk and moved them around, and at the same time as each of the arrangements were confirmed I changed the colours of relevant cells to green on my spreadsheet. Then the day finally arrived when I heard that I had a Chinese tourist visa in my passport. This was great news. I used to fret about the amount of detail required for a successful Russian visa application, but I think on balance they are easier to complete than the Chinese equivalent, which requires lots of backup documentation. I was now able to cancel all the dummy reservations, and my agent in London passed the red tape baton over to an officially approved Chinese travel agent who would apply for the permit allowing travel on the Tibetan Plateau. The rules seemed straightforward: once you had a visa, a guide and ground arrangements it was in the bag. As long, that is, as your plans didn't clash with any significant religious dates in the Chinese calendar, when without warning no permits would be issued to foreigners. I wondered if they were conducting background checks on me.

The Manchurian Candidate

I found a zipped ring binder to store all the paperwork that I would need to travel with. It grew comfortingly thick with reservations and official documents. When real tickets started to arrive through my letterbox, it was a sure sign it wasn't long until blast-off. Getting a ticket on the Trans-Mongolian and Trans-Siberian train can be tricky if you leave it too late, but I suspected there was no problem travelling through Manchuria, especially in the middle of winter – there would be few reasons for people to punish themselves with this route rather than the easier alternatives. I photocopied each ticket and also scanned them, as a backup. I attached these to an email that I would be able to access wherever I was in the world as long as it had the internet. The last thing to arrive back on my desk was my scruffy-looking passport. I read somewhere that well used passports were actually better than clean ones. Officials generally assume that a lived-in travel document was less likely to be a fake. On this basis I should be just fine. The red tape was complete.

Next I needed to decide what to take on this rail journey and, just as importantly, what to pack it into. Having nearly crippled myself with a giant-size duffel bag in 2014, for my next journey I'd then purchased a wheeled bag big enough for me to climb into. My resolve this time was to travel much lighter, and to find a bag with soft sides, so that I could wedge it into the varying sizes of the luggage spaces on sleeper trains. I have read about the supposed dimensions of the storage spaces under the seats on different trains, but in my experience no two trains are ever

The Railway to Heaven

alike. In the end I found a bag I liked in my local branch of a department store that never likes to be knowingly undersold. It had a pair of rugged wheels, lots of zips and big straps around the outside to compress the contents. On the top was an extending handle, and I worked out that I could use this to anchor a second, smaller bag. It didn't make me feel very much like an explorer, but at least I had something that I knew would be suited to my needs.

The new bag filled fast with all the usual practical items. First aid kit, thermos flask, winter boots, camera gear, plugs, adapters, batteries, tools, rope and tape. But it would be mad to head off without a jar of Marmite, a bag of jelly babies, some Coleman's mustard powder, and of course my trusty portable espresso machine. The only snag was I wasn't sure where my clothes would go. But after a few attempts, somehow it all squashed in. With my legs holding the bag down I heaved on a couple of compression straps until it looked like I might be carrying less than I actually was.

The spreadsheet for my journey, now complete with massive amounts of detail coloured mostly in green, was large enough to look like it might relate to the movement of an army brigade to a distant battlefield. But my diary was much simpler. Prior to my departure date, other than the dates for a few work meetings, there was just a day in December that said 'Tibet' and a long grey line spanning several weeks.

The Manchurian Candidate

My favourite armchair in Channings Hotel was a good place to read and further research my journeys. I got seriously inspired there; perhaps the spirit of Sir Ernest was rubbing off on me. I began to feel that anything might be possible. The afternoons flew by with several pots of Assam tea and a pile of books about the great railways of the world and the history of Tibet. Once you're out on the rails of the legendary Trans-Siberian, as you sit in a comfy modern climate-controlled carriage it's all too easy to forget about the history of its construction. You take it for granted. But it wasn't always that easy. The 9289-kilometre line from Moscow to Vladivostok was finished in 1890. More than 60,000 men had laboured on it under the supervision of Tsar Nicholas II, creating one continuous set of tracks across the vast expanse of Siberia. Then millions of migrants headed east on the line, opening the region up to agriculture and industry. Today it is still far cheaper to deliver a container from China to western Europe by train than it is by ship. Most people use the words 'Trans-Siberian' to mean any of the major routes – the original line to Vladivostok, the Trans-Manchurian to Beijing that opened in 1902, and the Trans-Mongolian to Beijing that was not finished until 1961. It is now actually possible to travel on a single train from Kiev to Vladivostok, a journey of over 11,000 kilometres – the longest continuous rail service in the world.

Other than its vast size and beauty, Siberia is perhaps best known for its brutal climate. But as a surprise to the unprepared, the summer can be quite hot, and the temperature variation between the seasonal highs and lows can range by over 100°C. The southern plains familiar to Trans-Siberian rail travellers have a relatively mild continental climate, with a longer, warmer summer than other parts of the region. Yet in winter at Irkutsk, near Lake Baikal, the average daytime January temperature is -20°C – but this can drop to -50°C. If you like your weather extreme, to the north and east is of Irkutsk lies the 'pole of cold', and at its heart a place called Oymyakon, best known for its record-breaking temperatures. Not for the climatic faint hearted, it ranges from +35°C in July to -67°C in January.

Fortunately, Russian Railways (RZD) have plenty of experience of operating in this climate. Their ability to run scheduled services across the continent in almost any weather is impressive to people like me who come from a country where leaves on the line or the wrong sort of snow are enough to cause widespread delays and cancellations. On board these trains, carriages are heated to close to 30°C inside, powered by both electricity and a coal-fired boiler. In winter it is quite normal to have a temperature difference of more than 60°C between your sleeping compartment and the other side of the thin metallic skin that separates you from the outside world.

But even the achievements of Russian Railways in this environment have been eclipsed. At the time of writing, the newest engineering marvel of the railway world is the

Qinghai–Tibet railway, which opened in 2006. At just under 2000 kilometres long, it manages to cross the mountains and permafrost of the Tibetan Plateau to reach Lhasa. At times more than 5000 metres above sea level, it has managed to overcome several major construction challenges. No less than 675 bridges have been built, and many tunnels at high altitude, one over 20 kilometres long. One of the biggest challenges to overcome was that the railway line has to sit on a semi-frozen layer that becomes unstable in the summer months. This crust would turn into mud beneath the trains were it not for the ammonia heat exchangers that have been drilled into the ground to keep it cool. Not only that, but long stretches of the rails run on bridges lifting the trains off the ground altogether, protecting the lines from heave and movement in the top layer. No wonder it took almost 22 years to build.

Then there is the train itself. It is no ordinary set of locomotive and carriages, but a purpose-built high-altitude trainset. Twin locomotives haul the carriages, which have shielded windows to protect their passengers from the extra-harmful radiation of the sun at altitude. Inside the air is enriched with oxygen to emulate a lower altitude and reduce the potential for altitude sickness. The compartment doors are semi-sealed to hold the air in and minimise pressure changes within the carriage. Underneath the train there is extra shielding to prevent damage from the ice and sand.

The Railway to Heaven

I make a few notes in my little book. 'Effects of altitude?', 'Drugs?' and 'Sun cream'. Travel to high altitude can be dangerous – but surely not in a train enriched with oxygen? It turns out that many get ill from the effects of the train's rapid climb to over 5000 metres. In contrast, mountain climbers ascend slowly, often returning to rest at lower altitude each night. Gradual gain in height means better acclimatisation. I did some climbs a few years ago and remember how I felt on the summit of Kilimanjaro. Gulping down mouthfuls of air, I progressed pitifully slowly – but I did continue to progress; many of those who had ascended more rapidly dropped out completely well before reaching the summit. The air pressure at the top is only about 40% of what it is at sea level, so the effective amount of oxygen in thethin air is much less. No wonder I was gulping air; I was having to breathe deeply to get perhaps half of what my lungs were used to. My eyes saw only saturated colours as the sun rose over Mount Kenya. I even had momentary out-of-body hallucinations as we reached the summit. But I made it.

So, how would this work out on a train? On this journey the 21% oxygen in the air at sea level would drop to around 11% effective oxygen at the Tanggula Pass on the Tibetan Plateau, around half what I was used to.

Many books have been written for mountaineers about the symptoms and treatment of altitude-related conditions. Most of the attention is understandably around acute mountain sickness, AMS. It ranges from a mild headache

The Manchurian Candidate

to something that can kill you though the conditions of high-altitude cerebral oedema (fluid around the brain) or high-altitude pulmonary oedema (fluid around the lungs). You might think that these conditions would only affect climbers on Mount Everest, but symptoms can kick in as low as 3000 metres. The way climbers manage to minimise the risk of getting AMS is to ascend slowly, take rest days, go back downhill to sleep at lower altitudes, and ascend no more than around 500 metres per day. Supplemental oxygen is a treatment, but not a solution; if you have acute AMS you need to get down, and fast. But on a train what do you do? There is no way of slowing the climb, and the ascent was going to be 5000 metres in a little over 48 hours.

Fortunately, there are several solutions to reduce risk and the effects of altitude sickness to the high-altitude rail adventurer. Oxygen was going to be available on the train, both generally as it was pumped into the carriages, and a 100% supply from your own bottle if you became unwell. Hydration was of course also easy – just drink lots of tea. By not physically exerting yourself, the chances were also reduced; after all, on the train there's no need to climb. Then there were the drugs: paracetemol or ibruprofen for general headaches, and diamox to minimise the symptoms, headaches and nausea. Mountain guides often disagree about the use of diamox (also known as acetazolamide), as it hides the symptoms of the conditions which could become life-threatening if not dealt with by descent. But for dealing with the symptoms it is highly effective.

The Railway to Heaven

So now I had to spend some time learning about the effects of altitude on the body. I read through several articles, noting things to expect like increased frequency of urination and a condition known as periodic breathing, which becomes common at 5000 metres. Because your body is breathing hard and deeply to suck in the air, it is also getting rid of carbon dioxide more efficiently than normal. It's actually getting rid of CO_2 that drives the normal pattern of breathing. But with much less CO_2 to get rid of, your body can stop breathing until it senses a need for more oxygen. This leads to a big gasp. Also, it can mean you wake up in the night feeling like you have stopped breathing. That is because for a very short period you have stopped breathing. In general, people moving to high altitude get poor sleep, and a couple of sources recommended using a sedative like temazapam. That sounded like a step too far me. Not only would I be comatose in the event of a situation arising, but drugs containing morphine or even codeine were a no go in the Russian Federation.

I started to read up on the effects of diet and altitude, too. I knew that even monks who were vegetarian often ate meat at altitude in order to get appropriate nutrition. But my medical dictionary suggested that carbohydrates were going to be better for me than protein at altitude – something to do with being easier to convert them into energy. It was sounding like noodles and sweet tea would be the mainstays of my meals on the plateau.

The Manchurian Candidate

My discovery that the train was equipped with ultra violet (UV) protected windows also got me thinking about what the sun might be capable of doing to my skin. For every 300 metres you gain in height, the UV radiation becomes on average 4% stronger. So at 5000 metres, UV is 66% stronger than at sea level. Packing note to self: big hat.

'Earth to Matthew!' Keith Parsons had arrived without my even noticing, and was playing with the chess pieces on the table between us. It was time for our weekly mentoring session; helpful questioning of my plans and a gentle stretching of my goals. 'More tea?' he asked, putting his glasses on and getting out his notebook and a pad of post-it notes.

Time always seems to slow down as a new adventure approaches, and I tend to get apprehensive about what I'm about to do. My mind becomes plagued with uncertainties, and also the big questions: Why am I doing this? What will I gain from it? Will the world continue to turn whilst I'm away? I try to counter this by reminding myself that once I set off I usually normalise life on the rails in a matter of days, and after a week or two I'm simply thriving on living each day at a time, with little concern for the past or the future. The day-to-day excitement of new experiences really are like a drug. I wish they could prescribe that degree of happiness and fulfilment on the NHS.

The scheduled day of my departure was fast approaching and I felt that I was in no man's land. No longer a normal

The Railway to Heaven

person with a normal job and a normal life – but not yet an adventurer, either. Kicking my heels, all I had left to do was recheck my paperwork and stare at the bag in the corner. I dared not play with it for fear I wouldn't be able to get everything back into it again. I was feeling pretty pleased to leave behind my life in this suburban world. I needed to get on with this.

Printed in Great Britain
by Amazon